THE OTHER AMERICA

THE OTHER AMERICA

Julia Mercedes Castilla

Copyright © 2013 by Julia Mercedes Castilla.

Library of Congress Control Number:	2013916454
ISBN: Hardcover	978-1-4836-9829-8
Softcover	978-1-4836-9828-1
Ebook	978-1-4836-9830-4

All rights reserved. No part of this book may be reproduced or transmitted in any form or by any means, electronic or mechanical, including photocopying, recording, or by any information storage and retrieval system, without permission in writing from the copyright owner.

This book was printed in the United States of America.

Rev. date: 10/17/2013

To order additional copies of this book, contact:
Xlibris LLC
1-888-795-4274
www.Xlibris.com
Orders@Xlibris.com

ACKNOWLEDGMENTS

I would like to thank my husband, Alberto, for the help he is always ready to give me, finding reference for everything I need and more. I also want to thank, Guida Jackson Hume, Ida Luttrell, Karen Stuyck, Vanessa Leggett, Jackie Pelham, Patsy Burk, Lynn Gonzales, Irene Bond and Louise Gaylord, dear writers and friends of many years, for their invaluable critiques and friendship.

CHAPTER I

WAS IT WRITTEN somewhere that I was not destined to spend most of my life in the home of my ancestors, or was it a twist of the wheel that shifted roads when I was not looking? I often think of the circumstances that uprooted me, my husband, and my descendants from the land, culture, family, and idiosyncrasies of my country and its people.

My name is Marcela and this is my story. Like many others, I found myself placed in another land as if moved by invisible hands in a predestined manner, far away from the world I knew as my own.

There is never an explanation for life's profound happenings. God must have wanted me to walk a different path in another place. That is what I tell myself when I think about the life my family would have lived had we stayed in the South American country we left years ago. This thought seems to surface when least expected. It makes me wonder how very different my life might have been. Sometimes I have fun elaborating on the many roles I could have played. At times my imagination goes wild. Being president of my country would not be far-fetched.

Believing, as I do, that each person has a destiny and a mission—unless free will detours you from it, which you can never confirm—my journey to a foreign country must have been written somewhere in the book of life.

My story begins the day before I left with my new husband, many suitcases and the naïveté of youthful inexperience.

May 23

I glance about me in the hope of imprinting inside my soul every detail of the home I have shared with my parents and siblings for many years. I detail my surroundings: the Louis XVI furniture my father inherited from his grandparents, the somber dining table and chairs where we ate as long as I can remember, paintings, pictures, and decorations, especially the Lladró on the table in the living room—a beautiful girl wearing a hat, in her hand a rose. How can I leave all this for a place where people don't even speak my language?

A whirl of happenings crowds my head. My wedding four months before and the preparations for a trip to the United States in pursuit of Pablo's graduate degree have kept my life in constant motion. Excitement and anticipation have carried me from day to day for months.

There is no time to ruminate on whatever waits for us halfway across the continent. The suitcases are ready, and the reality of a move to a distant country is tomorrow's agenda. It momentarily overwhelms me to the point of making me want to forget about such an unpredictable journey, to go back to what I know. Yet I look forward to a life I cannot possibly imagine.

"Dinner is ready," says Mama, leading about twenty members of my family to the dining room.

Moving like a robot, I follow. My grandmother's dishes with the tiny green leaves I so love set on my mother's favorite embroidered tablecloth, and a crystal vase filled with roses as a centerpiece make my heart swell with joy and sadness.

The idea of leaving everything familiar gives me a strange feeling, one I don't understand since we are coming back in a couple of years, after Pablo finishes his master's degree. I look at my new husband for comfort. He smiles nervously. We hold hands for a moment. I know he can hardly wait to begin his studies, and yet apprehension seems to be crawling about him, about both of us.

Papa, sitting at the head of the table, observes the faces of the guests in silence, his face strained, sober.

"You are going to have to learn to cook," says Aunt Magda, who, as the wife of a politician and an ambassador, has traveled the world and seldom has the need to do any cooking herself. "As students, you won't be able to have maids like you have here at home. Are you ready for that, Marcela?"

"I don't know." I have not thought about such trivialities. There are so many other wonderful things to do and see that cooking has not entered my mind.

"Better prepare yourself." Aunt Magda looks at me from across the table with pity, making me feel uncomfortable and incapable. "Taking care of a house is not easy."

I don't dwell on the matter. Cooking, ha! It's done all the time. Why worry about such a task? At that moment a maid, wearing a black uniform and a white organdy apron—used for special occasions—enters the room, carrying a big silver platter of food. This image would not be part of my daily living for a couple of years, making me think for a moment on how much my life will change.

"Are you sure Pablo's Fulbright Scholarship is going to be enough for your living expenses?" Papa asks in a low voice.

"Yes. Why do you keep asking about the scholarship?"

"Scholarships are never enough. Where are you going to get more money? How are you going to manage? You are so young and inexperienced, with a husband just a few years older. How can you . . . ?" Papa's eyes fill with tears he tries to conceal by averting his face.

"We were able to get additional funding for me," I say, hoping he wouldn't ask any more questions. We requested a student loan but have not received approval yet. Fibbing is not something I do often. Neither my grandmother, who was a saintly woman, nor the nuns who imbedded in my soul all the commandments ever written would have approved of my white lie.

My father looks at me with those piercing dark eyes, so much like mine, that have kept me from going against his wishes—most of the time. I began dating Pablo when I was very young, not quite thirteen, making my father most unhappy. So I openly defied him, straining our father-daughter relationship for months at a time. His eyes have a profound effect on me. They can look at me with the greatest love or intimidate me to tears.

"When did this happen? How come I don't know about it?" He keeps looking at me as if he could scrub my soul of whatever it is he cannot see.

"Yesterday. I haven't had time to talk to you about it."

"What are you mumbling there? Let us in on the conversation," jokes Aunt Magda's husband.

Papa doesn't say anything. He seems somewhat relieved.

"Just talking about the trip," I say, filling my mouth with a piece of *carne asada*.

My father's concern for my well-being both touches me and irritates me. It is time for him to let go, and yet it makes me feel loved. My life is full of ambivalence.

There are no more questions, but I can see concern written all over his face; or is it that he doesn't want me to go so far away from home? He believes I was too young to date, much less to marry. My leaving home seems beyond his endurance.

This dinner is not like the other farewell dinners and parties Pablo and I have attended for weeks. Family and friends have showered us with food, niceties, and advice. This is the last night I will spend with my family for the next two years. Somehow these two years seem long. Very long.

"Marcela, don't forget to write," says one of my cousins on her way out.

"I won't." When was dinner over? My mind has taken me to so many scenarios for my new life, I have missed what I could not retrieve, the sharing of the last few hours with my family.

"Everyone is gone." Mama holds me by the arm as we close the door after the last guest. Her big hazel eyes inspect me from head to toe as if she needs to remember how I look. "Come, let's sit in the study for a few minutes. Your father and Pablo are in the living room. I know you have to get up early, but a few minutes won't matter."

Being the first to break barriers and fight battles has been like a curse some evil spirit put on me without my knowledge. No one in my family has ever left home for a long time. Going to a foreign country was unthinkable. And, of course, I have to be the first to have a boyfriend, the first to marry, and now the first to go away, far away from home. Maybe one day I will be first to do something everyone thinks is wonderful instead of making people mad or sad.

Mama smoothes her black silk dress as she crosses her legs. "I am happy for you and Pablo and for the opportunity you have of seeing a different world, learning another language, another culture. I would have loved to do what you are going to do." She pauses for a moment. "It's hard to see you go so far away from home. You didn't give us much time to get used to the idea. Getting married and leaving your country in four months is a little too much. Don't you think? Your father is . . ."

Mama goes on for a long time. I don't register half of what she says. It pleases me to know she is happy for me. Most everything else, I expected her to say.

I give Mama a kiss. "I'm going to miss you more than you can imagine, but don't worry about us, we'll be all right. I better go now. It's late. Good night, Mama."

I go upstairs to my old room. A few minutes later Pablo follows me.

Soon the house is silent, lights out, hearts pounding. Anticipation, dread, and excitement own my being, making it impossible to sleep. Pablo holds me. The cold air of the night has covered the house, seeping through the bricks, chilling us both.

CHAPTER II

THAT I WAS once so young and so innocent is now hard for me to imagine. The passing of time has a way of changing all of that naïveté to a more practical, careful, and distrustful worldview. As I look back on the day we left, I see two confused youngsters who boarded the wrong plane on their way to meet their destiny.

Was it me, us, or some alter ego hidden in my past? Since I am now planted firmly here in my adopted country, it must have been me, getting off from the wrong aircraft, feeling quite stupid as Pablo rushed me to the plane that seemed to be miles away. Both of our families and close friends—more than twenty people—had come out to the airport to see us off. I still get teary-eyed remembering the embraces, the kisses, the emotions, the shrinking of the heart as we prepared to board.

May 24

A moment ago we said good-byes to family and friends. Are we really leaving our country, home, and family? If I am awake, we must be going somewhere, suitcases and all. In a daze, I follow Pablo to another plane, hopefully the right one this time.

My coat weighs a ton. Pablo's aunt had pinned to the inside of my overcoat a couple of handmade sweaters she believes we can't survive without. I drag two bags with items we just have to have.

Pablo grabs several bags and takes my hand, hurrying me.

"I can't run any faster," I say. "You go ahead. Have them wait for me." I had asthma as a child. Even though I seldom suffer with it anymore, when frazzled and distressed, I can hardly breathe.

Pablo stops running and seems to hesitate, walks a couple of steps, and backtracks. "Okay, but . . ."

"Go, before the plane takes off." I move away and begin to panic. Puffing and wheezing, I push myself forward.

I often dream that I am running away from someone or I need to go someplace I never seem to reach. Am I in one of those dreams where no matter how hard I try I never get there?

I don't know how I've made it on time. I have no recollection of the last few minutes, but somehow I stumble up the steps where Pablo is waiting for me. Moments later we find ourselves sitting in our seats. Slowly, I begin to breathe again.

"I bet the family was hysterical that we almost boarded the plane going to Caracas instead of Miami." I look out the small window toward the terminal building as if I could see through the glass and the walls that keep the members of my family away from me.

Pablo laughs. "Can you imagine the chaos there? It must have been a sight."

The comic scene in my mind relaxes the tension for a moment. I look for a place to put my coat. It's suffocating me.

Pablo opens each compartment in the plane until he finds one where he can squeeze in my coat and sweaters.

"Why are we taking all of this stuff with us?" Pablo's face is red, and his agitation is contagious. He goes on and on about dragging so many bags, coats, and jackets.

"There is not much we can do now. Sit and try to relax."

I wish I could follow my own advice. Pablo is the nervous kind, so I decide to get hold of myself and pretend to be calm, a feeling as foreign to me at the moment as the country we are heading to.

The engines roar—my heart and pulse roaring along with them. It is time. We are really leaving.

"Extinguish all cigarettes and buckle your seat belts, please," says the captain. A stewardess stopped by our seats.

I try to comply, but the shaking of my hands makes it difficult to insert one piece inside the other. The impatient woman throws herself across Pablo, mumbles something, buckles my belt, and leaves, still mumbling.

I must look more nervous than I think for the stewardess to believe that I can't buckle myself.

Pablo produces a smile that is more of a twist of the mouth. I think we are both so nervous it must show.

"You look like a ghost. Are you afraid?" The fact that he seems to be feeling as bad as I feel comforts me.

"I'm a little nervous," he says.

"More than a little," I say, teasing him.

He doesn't respond. The plane begins to move. The tears that I tried to repress when embracing my parents come back, rushing down my cheeks faster than I can wipe them off. I turn my face toward the window, trying to see in my mind the faces of my loved ones. What are they feeling? Are they still looking out the window? Have they gone home?

"Ladies and gentlemen, welcome to . . ." The stewardess goes on about the safety measures to take in case of emergency, making me tense all over again. I close my eyes and wait.

Butterflies flutter in my stomach, putting a stop to my tears for the moment. The plane takes off. I grip onto the arms of the seat with all my might, hold in my stomach, and begin to pray. What are we doing?

Neither of us seems to be in a talking mood. My emotions are in shreds, adding to the fear of flying I developed when I was twelve. Uncle Al and Aunt Magda took me on a trip in a small plane that shook so horribly I promised never to get on one of those again.

"Oh, God, please, help me." I have no idea what kind of help I want from the Almighty, but I need all the help I can get before I lose it. I don't trust metal birds at all.

Pablo looks at me but keeps quiet. He holds my hand. After a few bumpy minutes, we break through the heavy clouds that seem to go on forever. We finally make it to where I can see the blue sky.

Sometime later the captain announces that we are about to land.

"Why are we stopping in this city?" Pablo's voice startles me. "I thought it was a direct flight to Miami."

I peer out the tiny window. The clouds underneath look like whipped cream. I thought the stewardess was still talking. She made me so nervous I closed my mind and ears. "We are?"

"The captain just said so."

The plane jerks. "What's happening?" I barely utter the words when I feel the drop. I know we are going to crash. Terror grabs me by the throat.

"Your attention, please. We are experiencing crosswinds, not unusual for this region. Keep your seat belts fastened," says a voice over the intercom.

We go back to silence, unable to put our growing fear into words.

After a few minutes the plane flies smoothly. Relaxed, I close my eyes and bring back the happy memories of my wedding day.

It began with me sneezing uncontrollably. My allergies flared up more than ever. A bride with red eyes, blowing her nose and going achoo, walking down the aisle, was not a pretty picture. The more I worried about it, the worse it got.

In desperation Mama gave me a glass with half an inch of gin. "This is just medicine, and it does not taste good at all."

"Don't worry, Mama, I'm not planning to turn into an alcoholic." I drank the whole thing in one gulp. Soon I was feeling like a new person. I put on my white lace and tulle wedding gown. Mama fixed my veil on my head while I looked at myself in the mirror, reflecting someone who certainly didn't look like me.

The gin did the job. I hardly remember walking inside the church. It was as if I were walking on cotton or something very soft. Pablo said he wished he had done the same.

"We are ready to land." Pablo's voice brings me back.

The image of my dancing the first waltz with my father, then Pablo and almost every male in the family, comes to a halt at the reality of the approaching landing.

Fear takes over again. *I have to stop this silly feeling,* I tell myself, holding on to the seat. Maybe my father is right. We are too young to be going so far away from home.

We have to deplane unexpectedly, something about a delay. I'm glad I'm not wearing my coat. I forgot how hot it gets here on the coast. My stockings stick to my legs.

"We're going to miss the connection in Miami." The thought doesn't make me happy.

"I hope not. A Fulbright representative is waiting for us at the airport in Washington." Pablo paces.

We have been here for a long time. There is no way we can make the connection. What are we going to do? Worry creeps over me, tightening my muscles like the strings of a tuned guitar.

Pablo goes on pacing and doesn't say much.

"Passengers to Miami ready to board at the international gate."

We rush behind a man I recognize as a fellow traveler and don't stop to breathe until I find myself securely seated. I shut my eyes for a moment and wait for the aircraft to take us back up into the sky.

Pablo eases his arm behind me. "It's so good to be together on this trip. I never would have come alone."

I smile back. A warm feeling lifts my spirit. The sun is bright, and the flight smooth. Finally able to relax, I take a book from my bag and read for a while.

I wish I could go to sleep. We have been flying for hours, and I am ready to jump out of my skin.

"Welcome to Miami. I wish you . . ."

I don't hear the rest. I have gone back to holding the arms of the seat and clenching my teeth while the plane lands. I know I am a sensitive person, but I didn't expect to be this . . . I can't find a word to describe my own feelings and reactions.

I look at my watch. It's six thirty. We missed our connection.

CHAPTER III

RECALLING THE FIRST time I left my country gives me a feeling of melancholy. There are times when I long for the embrace of the land that welcomed me at birth. The land, so dear to one's heart, doesn't always turn out to be what is inside the folds of the mind, where lasting memories find refuge. Pablo and I have visited our country many times since then. We even went back to live there for several years but could never recapture the world we remembered.

Many happenings have shifted the kaleidoscope of the life I knew before boarding the plane that took Pablo and me to a country where we were all alone, without relatives or friends to help us. At the time it did not seem to register that we were on our own.

Searching into the depths of my stored memory, I find two figures bent over by the weight of the luggage they carried, walking slowly, and looking baffled. It is hard to identify those figures with the Pablo and Marcela of today.

May 24

We walk inside a crowded room. People scurry from place to place. We stop, trying to figure out where to go. I bite my lip to make sure it is me, entering a world that seems unreal. What a strange sensation. I shake my head and continue walking.

"American citizens this way. Others go to the left," says a woman in uniform. The only way I know what she says is because I read the signs in Spanish.

The lines are endless. We put the bags down and push them with our feet until we find ourselves in front of a desk where a sour-looking man frowns at us as if we were intruding into his space. He extends his hand.

I am the passports keeper. I figure that's what he wants, and we hand them to him. He stamps them, says something, and dismisses us.

We walk to a row of chairs. Pablo, his face flushed, drops the many bags he has hauled from one America to another. I can't feel my numb arms.

I collapse on the seat next to him. My mind blank, too tired to worry or think about the fact that we had missed our connection to Washington. As if hypnotized, I stare at the people going by, pulling suitcases, packages, children, as they rush to wherever they are going.

"I wonder how far the Avanta's counter is." Pablo seems to have revived enough to ask a question I can't answer. "Why don't I stay here with the luggage and you go find out. I don't want to leave you here alone with the bags."

He doesn't want to leave me alone but has no qualms about sending me out there. Why did he ever consider sending me to look for the airline counter? Doesn't he care? "You go. I'll wait here." I turned my face in a huff.

Pablo doesn't move. He seems to be debating with himself. Hesitantly, he takes a few steps, looks back, and finally disappears into the crowd.

I panic. My mind goes wild. We may not find each other again. What will I do? The idea of being left alone in a strange country gives me such a fright, I stop breathing for a moment.

"I hope he remembers where I am." A tall man, carrying a music instrument in a case, turns his head. I look away. I was not aware I had talked aloud.

Time goes by. Where is he? I search for a slender, five-foot-seven man, brown hair and eyes among the travelers, but even though many fit this description, neither of them is Pablo. How long before another panic attack sends me into a screaming fit? The bags keep me tied to my seat. As I get ready to grab my purse and leave my guardian angel in charge while I go look for my new husband, I see him running back.

"The next flight won't be until tomorrow at six thirty in the morning. They won't pay for a hotel, food, or anything." Pablo's dark hair, always neat and in place, is all over his face.

"It isn't our fault we missed the plane to Washington. They should pay." I'm glad our family gave us a little extra money.

Pablo says that not only do we have to pay for hotel, food, transportation and whatever else comes our way, but also we have to get the luggage, take it with us, and bring it back. The airline won't keep it here.

The thought of having to carry the huge suitcases we had packed with every item we could possibly need, plus everything we are already carrying, is more than I can take. Tears come rushing down my face. I want to be strong and resourceful, but I don't know how. *Papa is right,* my mind tells me. We aren't ready for the trials we are sure to encounter. It seems easier to go back to Papa than to face problems as adults. Right now I don't feel like an adult. I want someone to take care of me.

Frustration and anger feed the courage I don't have. I decide to go back to the airline again and see if I can talk them into helping us. I might as well learn to handle this kind of situation.

Pablo throws his arms in the air. "They're not going to help us. Why bother?"

"I just have to do it." I put on my coat and everything it contains, hang bags and purse from my shoulders and arms, and take off.

Pablo rushes behind me, pulling along his load.

After several stops along the way to shift bags and rest for a moment, we find ourselves across the counter from a man who doesn't seem to want to deal with us.

I want to turn around and forget it, but instead, surprising myself, I gather my fading courage and say in my native language, "We missed our connection because our plane was late. It's only fair that you pay for our hotel and dinner tonight. We're stranded."

"I already told the young man this airline doesn't pay for hotels. These delays happen. We would go broke if we paid passengers' expenses for every delay. I'm sorry, but there is nothing I can do."

I keep on arguing as I get angrier and angrier to the point of wanting to jump over the counter to strangle the man. He took a Lucky Strike cigarette from a package on his desk and calmly dismisses me by walking away. Feeling helpless, I turn to my husband, who kept quiet while I argued.

Pablo lowers his arms, along with several bags. "We'll just have to find a place to stay tonight."

I know he's right. These people won't help no matter what we do or say. I can't believe our airline refuses to help us in a strange land. For a few seconds we stand still, in total confusion. Where to ask?

"Sir, here is the name of a hotel very close to the airport. It is a good and inexpensive hotel." A young woman from the airline calls Pablo from behind the same desk, where the disagreeable man, who seems to have disappeared, stood moments before. "I'm sorry you missed your connecting flight. I wish I could help you." She talks softly as if she didn't want anyone but us to hear her. She gives my bewildered husband a piece of paper.

"I don't think it is right that . . ." The words coming out of my mouth don't find an audience. The woman lifts her shoulders, makes a face that tells me there is nothing else she can do, and walks away.

Pablo, his voice barely audible, lets me know there is no way we can carry everything to a hotel. It will be easier to spend the night sitting here than having to go through so much trouble. I don't comment. I don't want to think beyond the collecting of the suitcases. At this point I can only handle one thing at a time.

Pablo stands there, looking as if he is in shock, his blank face staring over a multitude of travelers going in all directions. "I think we go to Baggage, which comes from *bag*, English for *maleta*." He points up to the signs.

"Isn't *maleta* a suitcase?" I'm sure *bag* is the name given to something made out of plastic, paper, or cloth.

My high school English isn't going to help me much. I don't understand a word of what is echoing over the loudspeaker. Pablo had to take the TOEFL exam, so his knowledge of written English is better than mine. I can tell his understanding of the spoken language isn't good either.

We trail behind a group of travelers coming out from gate 8 to the baggage area.

I head for the closest chair, discombobulated, feeling as if another human being had taken residence inside my body. Pablo unloads himself and walks among the many wandering passengers in search of their belongings.

A few minutes later he appears, pushing two suitcases with his feet and carrying two in each arm. His red face doesn't reassure me.

"How can we possibly need all this? With so many people helping us at the airport, I didn't realize we have brought the whole country with us."

I understand his frustration and decide not to comment. I can't wait to go to a hotel. We need a good night's sleep.

In two carts we accommodate everything and head for customs, where they open every suitcase, leaving us with a mess.

With hands that refuse to work in an orderly manner, we stuff things back inside the suitcases the best we can, put them back in the carts, and go out the door to meet a city we can't imagine.

CHAPTER IV

TRAVELING HAS BEEN part of my life since the day I came to the United States, and yet I have never learned to travel light. No matter how I struggle to do it right, I always end up with huge bulging suitcases and more bags than we could possibly need, to the dismay of Pablo, who hates to carry luggage. It must have to do with that first trip. I guess I have never overcome the feeling of needing this and that. Perhaps I need to carry part of my home with me.

It is difficult to analyze one's feelings of yesterday when that person that you were is so different from the person you are today, and yet it seems that you were that person just a short while ago. Time does that to you as it slips out of one's hands in the blink of an eye.

Could it be possible that these many years have gone by since a very young Marcela followed Pablo to fulfill his dreams of acquiring advanced degrees? As I close my eyes and think of the day we arrived in Washington, the scenes are so real and immediate, I expect to open them at the airport, looking around for somebody to help us find our way to where we were supposed to go.

May 25

Today is Pablo's birthday, a day he thinks should be a holiday—at least for him—since on this day he refuses to do anything that doesn't please him. As a child he often got in trouble with the school principal because he wouldn't go to school on his birthday. This will be a different one for him. We just had time this morning for a Happy Birthday kiss.

"I don't think anyone is coming to meet us." Still, Pablo keeps on looking.

I want to tell him there is no way for them to know what flight we were taking today, so no one will be coming, but decide not to say anything. I know Pablo expects a miracle. "Do you have a telephone number?" I ask him, overwhelmed by the predicament we are in.

We stand a few steps past the gate that let us into another crowded airport. I don't have the energy to panic. The night before in Miami was a nightmare. It took two taxis and a lot of begging to take us to the hotel, where we barely slept a couple of hours before we had to get back to the airport in a small van the hotel provided.

Pablo hauls the stuff he is carrying and sits in the first seat he finds. He opens his briefcase and scrambles through his papers for a couple of minutes. He's so agitated. I know he can't find anything.

"Let me see."

Frustrated, he hands me letters and documents.

Breathe deep and concentrate, I tell myself, sending the appropriate signal to my brain in the hope that it will take. I sit by Pablo and begin the search.

"It says here in this letter: 'If you need to get in touch with me, please call.' It lists a couple of numbers." I hand the paper to Pablo. He is holding his head.

Before I can say anything, he is on his way to find a phone. I suddenly feel numb, strange. Again I have the sensation of not being myself but an observer of my own life at a moment in time.

As I usually do when I am in a crowd, I study the faces of those who hurry by me and wonder about the lives they lead, as I ask myself what lies ahead of me.

"I have the hotel's address." Pablo's voice interrupts my wondering.

He found out the Fulbright people in charge of the program had sent a person yesterday. They were waiting to hear from us but told Pablo they were sorry they didn't have anyone who could come today.

"We're on our own," he sighs.

There is nothing for me to say. I get up and walk toward the Baggage sign. We are now experts on following this particular sign. The idea of dragging the luggage again makes me want to go back to my seat and stay there forever.

THE OTHER AMERICA

After much pulling, kicking, and complaining—something we have been doing for two days—we manage to take everything to the curb. Miraculously, a large taxi stops. The driver rolls his eyes. I'm sure he can't believe the luggage alongside the curb belongs to us. He piles suitcases inside the trunk and in the backseat. Pablo squeezes and folds himself in the back. I sit in the front, along with two more small bags.

The trip through the city becomes a blur. Completely spaced out, I give up thinking and stare at the buildings until we arrive at our destination. The hotel is a big old house located on a wide avenue.

A chubby woman smiled widely from behind the desk. "Fulbright usually sends us their students. It's interesting having guests from all over the world."

I hardly hear her. All I want is to go to a room with a good bed and sleep for a year. A young man helps Pablo with the endless task of taking the luggage to our room, conveniently located down the hall.

May 26

I don't know what happened last night. I must have found a nightgown since I have one on when I wake in the morning. It takes me a few moments to place myself. When did we get here? The question rumbles in my head long enough to answer it, bringing back the trip and its travails. Pablo sleeps soundly beside me.

I jump out of bed and go to the window. A quiet morning greets me. The wide avenue is empty. A solitary car drives by. "What time is it?" I mumble. I look at my watch. It's 8:45. Shouldn't the street be packed with morning traffic?

"What are you doing there?" Pablo's voice startles me.

"What day is it? Everything is so quiet."

Pablo's eyes stare at the wall. "Isn't it Sunday?"

"That's why there is no traffic. I'm hungry. Let's have a good breakfast to celebrate your birthday."

Pablo stretches out. He seems happy to have the day off for a late birthday celebration and to get acquainted with our surroundings since we can't get in touch with anyone until tomorrow.

Even though I am still tired, I'm too curious to stay in bed. I rush to take a shower and get ready.

I can't wait to explore the city where we are to stay for a month and a half. Washington is the first stop for the summer orientation provided by Fulbright before Pablo starts working on his master's program at the University of Illinois in Urbana. In July we'll be traveling to Austin, Texas, for the rest of the summer—so many places and happenings ahead of us. Today is the beginning of a new and unexpected life for us.

"Did the food taste strange to you? They must have used the same oil for the eggs and the potatoes. They had the same flavor." I say as we leave the small restaurant the hotel had recommended.

"Yes, they had a very unusual flavor. We'll have to get used to a different life, and that includes the taste of food." Pablo tends to become philosophical at times.

After Mass at a church nearby, we head for a commercial area a few blocks from the hotel. It's warm. I take off the light jacket Mama had her seamstress make for me. The seamstress also made several summer dresses I must wear to look like a young lady should. I guess the heat is something else to get used to, which won't be easy for me since I don't like hot weather.

We arrive at a bustling business district. I am surprised to see mostly black people since I seldom saw them back home. They seem nice and jolly.

We continue walking. This is another new experience for me. I feel as if I have been put on Mars and have no idea how to react, so I don't say anything about it.

"Let's go have a hamburger. Hamburgers in this country are supposed to be the food to eat, and it is already lunchtime." A sign in front of a restaurant across the street has a big hamburger display on it.

Inside the restaurant there are only black people, looking at us as if we shouldn't be there. We point to a big hamburger on the menu on the wall and sit to eat it, along with the french fries that are handed to us. We feel as strange as the looks we are getting.

"This is great, and it tastes like it should," I mumble with my mouth half-full. Sandwiches aren't part of our diet. We usually eat a full meal for lunch. "I guess we'll be eating this kind of food a lot."

"Sometimes." Pablo fills his mouth with french fries.

Sometimes? I repeat the word in my head. Is he expecting a big meal for lunch every day? No way. Who is going to cook it? Not me. I decide not to put into words my worrisome thoughts. I can't see myself in the kitchen. I don't want to think about this.

I get up from the table, ready for a rest and some soul-searching. "Are we going to stay at the hotel the whole month and a half?" To change the subject seems like a good idea.

"I don't know. I'll find out tomorrow. They might have other accommodations for us." Pablo glances about. "Isn't it strange that we don't see any . . . ?"

"Yes." I don't know what else to say. I guess it's normal to feel awkward the first day in a new country, among people different from us.

We stop at an ice cream place, where we linger for a long time, tasting all the flavors. I overdo it with the different kinds of chocolate—my favorite.

The afternoon is almost gone by the time we get back to the hotel. It has been a most interesting and puzzling day. I ponder it. I don't like this uneasiness that makes me want to run away from people. I can't put into words what I don't understand, so I decided to leave the mulling for another time.

CHAPTER V

I BELIEVE THAT the difficulties encountered when I first arrived in the United States shaped me and probably made me a better, more down-to-earth person. I want to make sure that the struggles I come across in life have a purpose. A feeling of accomplishment fills the soul when applying this principle. The idea of wasting good suffering is not acceptable.

There is always that looking back with fondness at those moments of wonder, adjustment, troubles, the magic of love, and many other emotions impossible to describe that turn into memories and images one keeps forever.

May 27

I need someone else to turn to. We have each other, but an older and wiser person will be a big help in this new world. I just remembered that Mama gave me a piece of paper with the name of her friend's sister the day before we left.

In the morning I tell Pablo I'm going to call Inéz, who married a colonel in the army and has lived here in Washington for many years.

"Do you know her?" Pablo asks as he gets ready to call his contact.

"No, I don't, but I have known her sister Lydia since I was a child. You know her and her husband. They are at almost every social event my parents have. It'll be good to get acquainted with someone while we are here. They should be nice people."

"She's a stranger, same as everyone else here." Pablo doesn't like bothering people. He swears the two of us can face the world by ourselves.

"I still want to call her. We won't be so alone . . ."

He doesn't say anything and goes about buttoning his shirt. I'm still in bed, not quite recovered from the traveling ordeal and somewhat at odds with myself. I struggle with my feelings and jump out of bed.

"I'll go take a shower while you make your phone call."

He is shuffling papers and doesn't pay attention to me. Moments later I hear him trying to call and then I hear the door close. It takes me a while to get ready. I have to press my clothes. I use the top of a dresser to try to do the job with an iron I borrowed yesterday from the hotel. I do one side and the back wrinkles. It is an endless task. I do what I can and decide the job is impossible and put the dress on as is. After all, no one knows me. I look at myself in the mirror. There is something odd and unfamiliar in the image I see; even the white linen dress doesn't appear to be mine.

Why is Pablo taking so long? I keep on trying to comb my hair that refuses to do what I want.

Pablo rushes in, jolting me back from my hair problem. He comes with the news that he doesn't have to go to the university until tomorrow. Someone is picking him up in the morning. We have another day to ourselves.

"Before we go anywhere we should take some clothes out from the suitcases. Everything is wrinkled."

Pablo looks at me with that look that says "No way." I know he isn't going to spend the day unpacking, so I let it go. Instead I asked him why he had gone out to phone when he could have called from the room.

He goes on and on about the numbers and the letters on the telephone and how they had confused him, so he went to get help. He brings all kinds of information about the White House, the Capitol, and the monuments. We are all set do some touring.

"Let's call Inéz first." Without waiting for a response, I take the phone and dial.

"Mama's friend said she will pick us up here at five and will take us to her house for dinner." A good feeling invades me. We are not completely alone, at least in this other America I hardly begin to grasp.

Pablo seems surprised as if he does not expect Inéz to be real but a figment of my imagination.

After breakfast, at the same café where we went yesterday, we hop on a bus and rush from place to place. It's hard to retain everything I see. We are able to go inside a couple of rooms at the White House. The sense of history overpowers me. I can almost hear Abraham Lincoln's boots stamping at the front door.

I forget my apprehensions for the future and enjoy the sights as if we were on vacation. Lots of tourists walk alongside, with their cameras hanging from their necks and shoulders.

"This is a beautiful city. Do you know that it's built in the same shape as Paris?"

"Really?" I haven't been to Paris, so it doesn't mean much to me, but it's an interesting piece of information.

It's almost five when we arrive at the hotel, with barely enough time to freshen up, before Inéz shows up at the door. She is a tall, dark-haired woman, unlike her sister, who has light hair and blue eyes.

"Lydia mentioned in her last letter that you were coming soon. I didn't know you were so young. You're just children. How is your mother? Last time I was there—must have been ten years ago—Lydia invited a few friends and family members and . . ."

Inéz continues talking for a few minutes as if it is the thing to do. She suddenly stops. I don't know what to say. I'm not good at making conversation with someone I don't know. Pablo stands beside me without saying a word. I'm finding out that my husband turns mute in the company of people he doesn't know.

"Sit down, please." I point to a chair by the window.

"No, thank you. Let's go. My husband should be coming home soon."

Inéz tells us about the city while she drives. I try to assimilate what she is saying, but somehow I cannot. I'm thinking about so many things. I can't concentrate.

She stops in front of a white wooden house with a front porch, similar to many of the houses in the neighborhood. She asks us to come in and make ourselves at home.

We walk carefully as if we expect the floor to collapse. It's a nice house, what I think a white wooden house should look like in this country. A picture of it put in my head by the movies I watched back home almost every Sunday afternoon.

Inéz puts her purse on a table in the entrance hall. "Sit down and relax. I have to take care of a few things in the kitchen. Can I offer you something to drink?"

"Okay, thank you. Can I help you?" I know it is the right thing to say even though I don't feel equipped to do anything in the kitchen. I hope she doesn't ask me to cook.

"You can help me serve the drinks. Would you like some iced tea?"

"Yes, thank you." I follow her while I try to picture iced tea. The tea I am familiar with is served hot, usually in the early evening. I cannot imagine it with ice.

Inéz takes a pitcher from the refrigerator and pours a liquid the color of tea in a couple of tall glasses. "Do you like it with sugar and lemon?"

"Yes, thank you." I keep repeating these two words like an idiot. I might as well learn how to drink this beverage. I look at our hostess in complete bewilderment, not knowing what to do or say.

She gives me two glasses filled with the amber liquid and asks me to take one to Pablo.

Like an obedient child, I rush to the living room, where I find Pablo looking at the pictures on the wall. I explain about the drink and how people here drink tea in a glass with ice. "Strange, but it's probably good."

Pablo takes the glass without paying attention to what I say. "This is so awkward. We are imposing ourselves on people we don't know," he says almost to himself.

"It'll be okay. She seems nice. She's not a stranger, but the sister of Mama's best friend." I drink some of the tea. It tastes good and it's very refreshing.

We sit and look at the glasses we hold, waiting for Inéz to tell us what to do next. Unfamiliar situations make me uneasy, and Pablo is not helping any. I should again go and offer my help in the kitchen even if I am worthless. Leaving Pablo to deal with his own uneasiness, I gulp the rest of my tea and get up.

As I walk to the kitchen a jolly-looking older man comes in the house. I stop and backtrack to my seat in the living room. I don't want to meet him face-to-face. I hope he doesn't see me. What would I say to him?

He goes directly to the kitchen. Moments later they both come to meet us. "Marcela, this is my husband, Colonel Patrick Bell."

"Hi, welcome to America. We're here to help you." He says something else I cannot understand.

"Thank you. We appreciate your inviting us to your home." I say it slowly, thinking, *Why is he welcoming us to America?* I have lived in America all my life. This country is in North America. I come from a country in South America, but America nevertheless.

I don't pay much attention to what the colonel is saying to Pablo, who seems to be struggling to understand. What are we doing here? This question seems to be glued to my brain. I look around trying to place my inner self in the reality of the physical place my body occupies.

Somehow we manage to converse while the colonel drinks a couple of straight gins. We sip wine, and Inéz does a lot of translating. She suddenly stands up. "You all must be hungry. Let's go eat."

A dining room in the kitchen seems different, but on second thought, it makes sense since there are no maids to serve us. Our first homemade meal in this country tastes delicious. Chicken, mashed potatoes, green beans, and corn on the cob delight me on this unexpected evening.

Have we been in this country only a couple of days? It feels like an eternity. My own country seems to be far away in distance and time. Are we Pablo and Marcela? I can't answer anything, so I shut my mind and go from one moment to the next.

CHAPTER VI

*M*Y HOME—AND I have called many abodes in many cities and countries home—is my refuge, my private haven, a place where I can be by myself. I value the privacy and solitude found in the familiar atmosphere of the rooms and furnishings that please and warm my heart.

Like most writers I have always strived for quiet time to hear my thoughts and invite my muse to softly whisper in my ear the magic words that will write the story bearing my name instead of hers.

My children were horrified when one year Pablo asked me what I wanted for my birthday and I requested to be left alone in the house the whole day so I could write. I told them I would be very happy if they came back around five with a chocolate cake—since I am a chocoholic. Then I would really enjoy a special time with them. I did like that year's birthday present.

May 27

Having to smile and be polite for hours can be trying sometimes. When this happens, I can't wait to be myself. Tonight, during dinner with Inéz and her husband, is one of these times. But I don't feel like myself now, not the *me* I used to be. I hope this feeling of being a stranger inside my body goes away. I can't have some other being inside me for two years.

Out of the blue, as we get ready to go back to the hotel, Inéz says, "Since you're going to be here for over a month, why don't you stay in the basement's little apartment. You can come and go as you please since it has a separate entrance. It's not connected to the house."

We look at each other in amazement. During dinner we have told our hosts that we'll probably be looking for an apartment close to the American University.

"We would not think of imposing," Pablo says. "We don't mean to—"

"Let's go down." Inéz interrupts him. "There is a room and a bathroom, and also a two-burner stove you can use. It's not what you're accustomed to, but it'll do for a short stay. No point in spending money on an apartment when we have room here."

I'm speechless. What can I tell these people we have just met and who are inviting us to stay in their home? Does Inéz feel she has to do it because of her sister's friendship to my mother?

We go out the main door and down several steps to the basement. Inéz turns the light on. We enter a big room filled with odds and ends, but I see mostly cases and cases of gin and vodka. She doesn't explain. I wonder if the colonel agrees with his wife's generosity. He's still upstairs, enjoying another drink.

In the back there is a small room with a bed, barely big enough for two. A narrow window in the upper part of the wall, level with the ground, lets in some light. It's not what I had in mind for our first love nest, but it would save us some money. The scholarship living allowance is not too big. Besides, I wouldn't know how to say no to Inéz.

Pablo keeps on trying to convey his opinion silently in language I can't understand, but it seems to me he's not too sure about the comfort of our new living quarters. I agree with him.

It's settled. Inéz will pick us up tomorrow evening since she doesn't have enough time to do it in the morning before going to work.

In a quiet mood we drive to our hotel. "Where do you work?" I say, breaking the silence enveloping us.

"I work at the United Nations." She doesn't elaborate.

I'm impressed. The United Nations sounds so sophisticated and international.

As we walk inside our hotel room, Pablo says, "Marcela, I don't know. That basement is dark and dreary. It's going to be bad for you. I'll be at the university every day, but you'll be staying most of the day in that hole. We better get a small place aboveground."

"It won't be so bad. It's only for a month. I don't want her to think the place is not good enough for us. She means well. And we'll have friends to help us when we need them. How can we tell them we don't want to accept their offer?"

"If you can stand the place, I guess it is okay with me." Pablo flops in the chair by the window. "I'm glad we didn't unpack."

While I get myself ready for bed, I ponder about the unexpected happening of the day. Basements are barely part of my vocabulary. There are no such places in the houses in my country. How could I ever contemplate such a possibility for a place to live?

May 28

Pablo is ready ten minutes before his ride arrives. "I'll try to be here before five. I'll let the hotel know we're leaving this evening. Be careful and don't go far." He gives me a kiss and a hug and leaves.

For the first time I find myself completely alone in a place I don't belong, with people I hardly understand. A feeling of abandonment weighs me down for such a long time, I fall asleep.

It's ten o'clock in the morning when I come to from a sleep so deep I can't move. I know it's ten because there is a clock on the table by the bed.

I try to organize the day in my mind. What am I supposed to do? I finally get up, put a Do Not Disturb sign outside the door, and get ready. *Ready for what?* I keep asking myself.

I don't want to go to breakfast alone, so I don't eat. I put back in the suitcases the few items we had unpacked. Before noon everything is ready for the move to Inéz's basement. My stomach is making noises. I need to eat something, but I don't know where to go. A grocery store. Yes, that's it. I can buy something and eat it here.

The woman at the front desk tells me there is a small store three blocks away.

Traffic is light and the street empty. It gives me a weird feeling. I keep looking back, expecting to see someone behind me. A strange notion since I have no reason to think this way.

I'm back in my room. It's nice to see the bed made and the room organized. It wasn't easy to find food I don't have to prepare. I put a bag of potato chips, an apple, and some kind of cake wrapped in cellophane on the dresser. This lunch is what Papa calls not a proper meal for one of God's children. If his food is not prepared the way he likes, he announces that the food is not fit, gets up, and leaves the table. I'm so hungry I don't care. I enjoy every bite.

I turn on the TV. I don't understand much. Tired of trying to catch up with the last word when I'm figuring out the first makes me turn it off. It's too much of an effort to try to follow. Maybe later when I'm in the right frame of mind. It's a good teaching tool if I want to get on top of this crazy language.

Uneasiness takes hold of me and I pace the room, getting all worked up. "Get hold of yourself, Marcela. Keep calm. You're not used to being alone in a foreign country, trapped in a hotel room," my sensible self tells me. I have a lot of growing up to do, so I might as well begin the journey. I take a couple of pages from the hotel stationery and begin writing a letter to my mother.

When Pablo opens the door, I'm still writing the longest letter ever. I didn't have to write many letters in the past since most everyone I know lived close-by. It's going to be different now. I'll have to write to family and friends. It'll be nice to receive correspondence from home. That idea makes me all gooey inside with the sweetness of anticipation. I'm glad we have an address now so I can begin getting letters soon.

"How was your day?" Pablo kisses me on the back of my neck as I finish writing the last sentence. He tickles me, making me laugh.

"Boring. How about yours? I'm sure it was more exciting than mine."

"A little confusing, lots of orientation meetings and getting acquainted with students and professors. There are students from all over Latin America. It was an interesting day."

I tell him about my uneventful day while he closes a couple of suitcases and piles them up by the door. Then we hear a knock.

Inéz parks the car in front of her house and runs up the steps. "Take your time unloading while I prepare supper. I already opened the door for you."

At the hotel it took us over half an hour and a lot of sweat to put everything in the car. Unloading isn't going to be any easier. We run back and forth to the car a million times, or so it seems.

About an hour later, with wet, shiny faces and tired bodies, we climb the five steps to street level and then another three to the front door to a home-cooked meal.

"Thank you, Inéz, you're a great cook. Dinner was wonderful. It's very nice of you to invite us to stay here." I feel I should say something profound, but I can't think of anything.

"There is no need to thank me. I'm glad you can use the basement. Let me know if you need anything. There is a store . . ." She tells us where we can get groceries and catch the bus and other important matters. She walks us outside and gives us the keys to the basement. "Good night." Inéz turns around and leaves us at the entrance of our new home.

Home, a safe place, a private heaven where a person or family dwells. How can we make a home out of this dark room that looks more like a jail in a dungeon than the living quarters of a newlywed couple?

CHAPTER VII

BREAKING INTO A new group of people has never been easy for me. A feeling of inadequacy grabs me with a vengeance. It takes me forever to feel comfortable with those I don't know. The tendency to turn into an invisible being is sometimes stronger than my good intentions to act like everyone else, cool and collected.

The more one dislikes something, the more it seems to be part of one's life. Meeting new people has become the norm for my family. Life has taken us to many cities and countries around the world, to new and different societies we had to adjust to, whether we liked it or not. It is still difficult, but I have learned to take it with a grain of salt.

However, belonging to big groups still overwhelms me, but I do a lot better than Pablo who gets claustrophobic in a crowded church.

May 31

It has been almost a week since we moved to Inéz's basement, and I am ready to jump in the lake. I don't know what I am doing in this faraway country. I miss my family and my friends so much I want to forget about everything and take the next flight home.

When I go to the store, I see older people sitting on their front porches with their chairs against the wall, looking at me strangely and saying things behind my back. I know they do. There is an old black woman with no teeth who greets me every time I go by her house. She seems nice, and I usually wave to her but I don't stop, and I don't know why.

I am pacing around the room, when I hear Pablo coming down the steps. I rush to open the door. "You're late, and I bought chicken for tonight's dinner. I hope it turns out well. I'm tired of canned food."

"Sounds good. It's getting warmer, and the bus stop is a couple of blocks from here. I'm going to take a shower. Did you really cook chicken? Did Inéz tell you how?" He looks at me with a silly smile on his face. We both tried to fry eggs for breakfast on Sunday and ended with burnt whites and runny yolks.

This is the first time I've tried to cook anything, but does he really think I am that incapable? I voice my displeasure and tell him I haven't seen Inéz in a couple of days. I have purposely stayed away from her. I don't want her to think I am fishing for another invitation to dinner.

"I'm sure it's very good. I'll be right out." Pablo disappears into the tiny bathroom.

I wish I had some rice to go with the chicken, but Mama hasn't answered my letter with the recipe. It'll be chicken with canned peas and a piece of bread. The chicken looks good, nice and brown. I set the wooden table outside the bedroom. We appropriated an area of the basement where I had placed the two-burner stove and the table, which looks as if it had been used as a tool table decorated with grease stains, dents, and scratches. I take a couple of napkins and use them as place mats to cover the stains.

It is a big deal for me to have gotten enough courage to cook drumsticks—all we can afford. I smile at the thought of our families sitting at such a table to eat dinner. They could not possibly imagine. I wrote Mama telling her we were staying with Inéz and her husband but gave no specific details.

Pablo, looking fresh and cool in his beige pants and blue shirt, sits on a three-legged stool. I have the privilege of sitting in the only chair in the basement, a wooden one that once must have been painted white. Inéz provided us with a couple of pots, a frypan, two glasses, dishes, and silverware.

I cut a piece of meat, and a trickle of a reddish liquid rushes out. I look at Pablo. He hasn't cut his yet. I don't say anything. Perhaps his chicken is well done. I wait in expectation. He's looking down, fork and knife in hand, ready to cut.

"I think it's raw inside." He puts the silverware down.

"But it looks brown outside. Doesn't it look done?" I want to cry.

Pablo pokes the meat with the knife. Watery blood splashes on the plate. "It looks okay on the outside, but what do I know? I have never cooked anything."

We look at each other in dismay. I want to cry but find it ridiculous to spill tears over raw chicken.

"We can go get a hamburger," Pablo says, getting up.

"Might as well because there is nothing else to eat." Since there is no refrigerator down here, I'm going to the store every day. Until Mama sends recipes, we will have to go back to canned food. Pablo likes canned soups anyway.

I don't know what to do with the chicken. I hate to throw it out, but I have no choice since I don't know how to cook it and cannot leave it out overnight. I put it in a plastic bag and, on our way out, dump the fruit of my labor in the garbage can outside the door.

"Do you think I'll ever learn how to cook?" I ask Pablo while we fill our mouths with juicy hamburgers at a small hamburger restaurant a few blocks away. "Too bad we can't eat out every day."

Pablo laughs. "No such luck. Don't worry, you'll learn. Every married woman has done it for centuries and a few men too."

"You wouldn't be one of those few men, would you?"

"I don't think so. But you never know." He goes on eating, leaving me to guess if he would even try.

It doesn't seem like a possibility, at least for now. Men in Latin America don't cook. It is a cultural fact. The image of my father, uncles, or any other man I know in the kitchen is not one I could put together. With Pablo I have hopes that in a couple of years, maybe . . .

June 7

The days are longer, giving us extra time to get to tour the city after Pablo comes home from school. This morning I received two letters, one from Mama with a couple of recipes I'm dying to try, the other from Pablo's aunt, Tía María. I read them over and over until my eyes fill with tears and I can't make out the letters anymore. My heart hurts from being homesick. It takes me the whole afternoon to pull myself out of the claws of depression.

Tonight we are invited to a dinner at a club, organized by the Fulbright Program. I can't wait. It has been so long since we went anywhere where we had to socialize. I'm sure I don't know how to talk to people anymore. Inéz and the colonel invite us to supper about once a week—giving us a respite from canned food—but it is not the same as going to a dinner party. The colonel doesn't talk much, too busy with his vodka for idle conversation.

I choose a blue skirt with tiny flowers and a white blouse for the occasion, glad to have the opportunity to wear my trousseau. If we had to carry all that weight from country to country, I might as well get to wear what I brought.

"You look very pretty," Pablo says as we wait in front of the house for our ride.

Before I can answer, a dark-blue car stops in front of us. An older man and his wife greet us.

"Welcome to Washington and to America," says the man as we jump in the backseat.

Here we go again. I guess America means United States. I don't understand why. We exchange greetings and smiles, and soon we are on our way to our first social event in this other America.

My mind goes back to the many social gatherings I've attended in the last few years. I danced the night away at many parties, went to delightful dinners at friends' homes, and participated in a whirl of events that now seem so remote I doubt I was ever there. Has my life changed so drastically that I can't identify with my old self? Deep inside I know this experience will help me mature, so I should be grateful for the opportunity. In expectation I walk inside a very nice restaurant for my first social event in this country.

CHAPTER VIII

MY MOTHER OFTEN said I was like an eggshell that breaks if you barely touch it. As a child I went through two bouts of pneumonia, one bronchopneumonia, all the childhood diseases at once, colds and whatever was going around. Asthma got hold of my body for several years. As an adult I had to acquire a heartier constitution so I could raise three children and take care of everything else.

If there is a time when you need your mother, it is when you are sick. It isn't easy to let go of the comfort of a mother's kiss when you don't feel well. The child in me surfaces with undignified furor when any kind of illness knocks at my door. I always crave the shredded beef broth with cilantro that Mama used to give me when I was ill. It doesn't taste the same if you have to drag yourself to the kitchen and cook it.

I can still feel the fear and abandonment the first time I got sick in the United States. It is strange to feel it so deeply as if it were happening now.

June 18

It seems that each day brings unforeseen experiences. At the party a few days ago, a woman asked me to taste her ice cream with the same spoon she was using. Yuck! It's going to take me a long time to figure out the customs and people in this country.

Two more weeks to go and we'll be on our way to Austin, Texas. Will it be similar to Washington? According to Pablo, Texas is a different world. I don't know if I can handle another world in such a short time.

"I'm glad we can eat rice now." Pablo smiles as he puts a forkful of white, fluffy rice in his mouth.

I smile back, pleased with my cooking success. It took me the whole week to get it right. I followed Mama's recipe step-by-step. Pablo didn't say anything, but it was mushy the first few times. I think I was using too much water. I didn't realize that the altitude changes cooking times and amounts. Inéz told me this important piece of news. Now that I've mastered rice, I'm going to try the spaghetti recipe.

"You got it right today. It tastes great. I enjoyed it even when it was mushy. I can handle it better than raw chicken. Why aren't you eating? You barely served yourself any food."

"I have cooked rice for so long that I'm not hungry now. I'm psychologically stuffed." I lift the fork with a few grains to my mouth but put it right back on the plate. I can't swallow anything.

"You haven't eaten much the last couple of days." With a concerned look, Pablo touches my forehead. I like that. It makes me feel special.

At night I can't sleep. I feel as if I had eaten half a cow. I get up and look for the antacid Mama made sure I packed. I can't find it in the dark.

"What are you doing? Are you feeling sick?" Pablo turns the light on.

"I don't feel too good. I don't know what I ate that is making me sick. I had canned stew for lunch. I hope it wasn't bad."

The medicine alleviates my discomfort, and soon I'm lost to the world. I'm okay in the morning, but after Pablo leaves, my stomach starts acting up. Could I be pregnant? Nah. It's probably something I ate.

June 20

A couple of days later I find myself throwing up, miserable with stomach cramps. When Pablo comes in the evening, I'm folded over on the bed.

"Are you feeling bad again?" Pablo throws his papers at the bottom of the bed and sits by me. "I think you should go to the doctor. I'll find one and make an appointment."

I don't say much. I don't feel like talking. All I want is my mother's shredded beef soup. It always makes me feel better. I mention the soup to Pablo. He looks dismayed at the idea of having to prepare such a potion.

I don't expect him to cook it since neither of us knows how. I miss being home so Mama can take care of me. I don't want to hurt Pablo's feelings, but mothers are a must when you don't feel well.

"I'm going to ask Inéz. She should be home now. I'll be right back."

Inéz sends a couple of tablets, broth, toast, and herb tea. It isn't Mama's soup, but it does help. It takes me all evening to eat half a piece of toast and a few spoonfuls of broth. By nine, I am exhausted.

June 21

After a fretful night and a long morning waiting for Pablo to let me know about the doctor, he finally shows up at one o'clock.

"The appointment is at three thirty. A professor at the university called the doctor's office and told him it was urgent. Inéz's doctor was out of town. Do you want something to eat?"

"I warmed up the tea. I've been drinking it all morning. You can open a can of soup." I send him to fend for himself while I get ready.

Facing a strange doctor who is going to speak to me in a foreign language is making me nervous while we wait in a room with other people. I wish I were seeing Dr. Pardo, who had been my doctor since I can remember.

I can hardly understand my name when someone calls me. I get up and walk toward the voice behind a door. Pablo stays in the waiting room. A nurse ushers me to a small room where she takes my blood pressure and my temperature and asks me a few questions. Half of them I can't answer because I don't understand them. She gives me a green gown to wear and disappears.

When the doctor comes, I'm shaking; I don't know if from the air-conditioning or from fear.

"Buenas tardes," he greets me with a big smile.

"You speak Spanish." I'm so relieved. It's bad enough to be sick and then to have to struggle with a language you hardly understand.

"Tell me a little about yourself and the reason you are here, trembling like a cold bird."

He writes what I tell him about my childhood illnesses and the symptoms that I have. He then examines me. I don't like it one bit. I want to run, but I can't move, trapped on top of the table.

"Don't look so worried. Get dressed. I'll be back soon. I need to run a test."

I wait for a long time before he comes back with a folder in his hand.

"Well, young lady, you are perfectly fine. You are not pregnant. You need to learn to cook real food. This is an order. You are not used to eating canned food, and the preservatives are bothering your stomach." He goes on with a scientific explanation of why my stomach rejects what is foreign to it and then hands me a prescription.

It's good to know I'm not really ill, and a baby can wait for a little while. I haven't thought much about babies. They will surely come in good time. We stop to get the prescription filled and go on to face the rest of the day.

June 28

I am back to normal. My cooking is improving some, but if I don't learn to cook, we are going to have rice coming out of our ears. Besides mastering the preparation of rice, I can now do hard-boiled eggs, so-so spaghetti, and very thin pieces of beef called minute steak. It's so thin I don't worry about it being raw. However, eggs are for breakfast and the thin steaks are a rarity, so rice is still our everyday dinner.

Every time I think of something I could prepare, I write Mama and ask her for the recipe, but it takes so long for letters to come and go that it's going to be quite some time before I learn to cook a few decent, edible dishes.

July 3

Our time in Washington comes to an end today. In a few hours we'll be on our way to Texas. Last night Inéz and the colonel invited us to a farewell dinner. This morning I got up early to finish packing. I'm trying to shove more clothes inside the suitcases. Pablo is struggling with his own packing. The idea of having to haul the luggage again is not appealing at all.

"You have been most kind to us, and we are very grateful for your letting us use the basement apartment," I say as we leave our good friends. "It would have been most difficult for us without your help."

"We were glad to do it." Inéz gives me a hug and turns to hug Pablo.

The colonel bows, dressed in his army uniform, then extends his hand, first to Pablo and then to me. He is an army man. "Have a good trip," he says and goes back to his chair and his gin or vodka; I can't distinguish one from the other.

It is late in the afternoon when a driver with a big car comes to pick us up and takes us to the bus station. Pablo must have told the taxi company we needed extra room for our luggage. The man doesn't look happy and barely talks to us after helping Pablo lift the heavy bags.

"We're going to have to do something about this luggage. We can't carry all of it from state to state." Pablo's red face looks at me as if I could make everything disappear. "After Texas we're going to Illinois. What are we going to do with all of this?"

"I don't know, but after carrying all of it halfway across the world, we can't just dispose of it. Besides, we need everything." I'm not good at getting rid of things. I tend to keep all kinds of stuff even if I don't need it because one day I might.

This is the first time I've traveled by bus that is not a school or city bus. With the allowance we have, we can only afford to travel by Greyhound.

"Are you carrying all your possessions with you?" asks the bus driver. "I've never seen anybody taking so much stuff."

Somehow we manage to put most everything in the belly of the bus. We find seats toward the back of the vehicle, which I don't like. I hope I don't get sick. I usually do when I travel by car.

Pablo must have read my mind because he asks me to sit by the window and tells me to relax and not to worry. He says that in this country most roads are straight, not like the ones at home, winding around the mountains, so I should be all right. He holds my hand as we wait for the bus to begin a three-day trip to Austin.

I don't know how to go about relaxing. I'm finding out I'm a worrier and have always been one. When I think about my earlier life, I see how tense and anxious I became during finals, illnesses, and dangerous situations. This is another matter I need to deal with, and it won't be easy.

CHAPTER IX

AS A CHILD I hated traveling by car. Papa was always dragging us out of bed at the most ungodly hour. He liked to be on the road before the sun came up. I could never figure out why. I remember being sleepy, hungry, and very cranky. I don't do any better as an adult. Sitting in a vehicle for a long time almost makes me sick.

The sad part of traveling is leaving part of you behind, days and moments never to be again. A feeling of loss stays with me for a long time after leaving a place, a town, people, events, and happenings that at one time were part of my daily living. Remembering good times and even bad times in the places I have once called home brings joy and sadness to my heart.

Yet the experiences encountered at each destination were extraordinary and unique. Looking back at the different places where we have lived feels like reliving one life at a time, which happens to have been lived by me.

July 3

Do most people take their surroundings for granted, or is it that the familiarity of it all becomes part of life itself? I'm now aware of everything and everyone around me, like a child discovering the universe from the window of a bus.

For a while I entertain myself, looking out as towns and open fields appear and disappear from my view as we move from state to state. These towns look nice, pretty, and neat but somehow remote. I'm used to seeing lots of people walking in all directions. Where are the inhabitants here? There is an eerie quietness about the towns we pass.

"Are you okay?" Pablo asks. "You are not very talkative."

"I'm just thinking about the differences in how people go about life here. I wonder if we can become like them."

Soon we are deep into a philosophical discussion about cultural behavior. It helps pass the time. Night arrives, covering everything, hiding nature and buildings from my view.

The bus comes to a stop at an illuminated site where a flashing neon sign announces a place to eat.

"We'll be here for forty-five minutes. Food and services are available inside. Use the rear door, please," says the driver through a microphone. "I won't wait for anybody, so please be on time."

We walk inside a cafeteria-style place. The door opens and closes constantly. The smell of greasy food nauseates me. I see a long line ahead.

I tell Pablo I know there isn't enough time for us to eat. I'm not hungry anyway.

"We better eat something. Who knows when we'll stop for food again. We'll be on the road all night." Pablo's voice sounds tired.

The lines are not any shorter in the restrooms. It is a race against the clock. We decide on two ham and cheese sandwiches and two Cokes we take with us, since there are only five minutes left before the bus resumes its journey.

Time goes by so slowly I decide not to look at my watch anymore. I finish my sandwich and try to sleep. Most of our fellow passengers are in a slumber state, including Pablo. I'm uncomfortable and can't find a good position. I wish I could read but it's dark. I will probably get sick if I do.

I'm hot. I'm cold. I wiggle in my seat. Soon I predict I may jump out the bus window. I've never been inside a vehicle for so many hours. Every so often the lights of a sleepy town break the monotony as I eagerly peek out the window, expecting to see something interesting. But most of what I see is pretty much the same in each town: gasoline stations everywhere, small businesses and buildings I can't make out in the dark.

"Why don't you sleep?" Pablo opens his eyes long enough to ask the question. Without waiting for an answer, he turns his head and goes back to sleep.

July 4

The day goes by without much more than a "HAPPY FOURTH OF JULY!" from the driver. I see lots of flags along the way to mark this country's special day. I guess there isn't much else you can see from a bus. We stop to eat breakfast, lunch, and dinner. I don't know how I have managed to stay put. Every time the bus stops, I want to get off and run away. It is a long, long day and night.

July 5

I must have dozed off for a while because, when I open my eyes, the sun is flirting with darkness on the horizon. It has been some time since I've been awake at sunrise. It is a fascinating sight that keeps me looking at it for a long time.

The rustle and mumble of fellow passengers slowly coming back to the awareness of a new day bring me to the present. For a moment I'm sure I'm back at my family's hacienda, where sunrises and sundowns are magnificent. I guess they are like that everywhere because this one is certainly beautiful.

Pablo sits straight and looks around as if to orient himself. "Did you get any sleep?"

"I don't know if I slept at all, just dozed off in the early morning. You, on the other hand, slept like a baby."

Another restaurant awaits us for breakfast. When I stand, I feel my skin—where it received the torment of so many hours against the seat—stuck to my clothing. It hurts, and I'm afraid it will peel, along with the garment attached to it.

"What's the matter? You're making such a face." Pablo stretches.

"I think my skin has taken a beating." I don't explain and he leaves it at that, too uncomfortable and hungry to bother his curiosity.

Scrambled eggs never tasted so good, and moving around is a real pleasure. However, going back inside the bus is trying. I have to sit lopsided on account of my wounded skin. We still have several hours ahead of us. I'm so uncomfortable this time. I consider getting off the bus and staying right there; but of course that is out of the question.

Pablo puts his arm around me. "Why don't you try to sleep? You look exhausted. You haven't slept much the last two nights."

His concern makes me happy enough to make myself endure the rest of the trip. It won't be easy in this position, but I'll do my best.

Of course I can't sleep. The air-conditioning in the bus is too cold. I wish I were wearing pants instead of a dress. Mama's standards, imbedded deeply inside me, prevail. "You don't leave the house if you are not properly dressed," she told my siblings and me over and over. "When you travel, you wear a nice-looking outfit."

I ask Pablo to get me something to wear over my legs. He stands on the seat and struggles with the many bags in the overhead rack. He finds his pajama bottoms and hands them to me.

Late in the afternoon the long trip finally comes to an end. The driver announces our arrival at the capital of Texas.

I'd give anything for a hot shower and a good bed. If I don't rest soon, I'll go out of my mind. I could sleep for a year.

We make our way down from the bus. Pablo rushes to rescue the luggage that seems to get heavier and bigger by the minute. We pull the suitcases and bags against a bench while we look for the person in charge of the program who is taking us to another unknown leg of our adventurous journey. It's hot, hotter than I ever expect any place to be.

"Mr. and Mrs. Almán? I am Jim Grand. This is my wife, Emily. Welcome to Texas," says a tall man approaching us, followed by a woman half his size.

The four of us manage to stuff the luggage in the back of their station wagon and backseat. Strong tall Mr. Grand hauls most of the luggage with great ease but with a strained face.

"You must be planning to stay here forever," says Mr. Grand as he piles up the last bag, blocking the rear view, which I'm sure annoys him.

Neither of us answers. Pablo plays deaf, and I smile. I don't have the energy to find an answer in my numb brain. It's not a good beginning in Texas, but we can't help it. We climb into the small area the luggage didn't swallow, in the backseat, sitting almost on top of each other. I lean against my good side.

"Do you have towels, sheets, dishes, glasses, and kitchen utensils?" Emily asks as we turn a corner onto a wide avenue.

"They probably have all of it and more inside those suitcases," Mr. Grand says.

"No, we don't." I volunteer the information, annoyed at the remark. In Washington, Inéz had provided all these items for us.

"Of course you don't." Emily turns to us and extends her hand to pat my shoulder as if she were apologizing for her husband's comment. "The apartment we got for you is furnished, but it doesn't have those items."

I keep on smiling since I don't know what to say. I don't know how I can coerce my brain into overtime. My eyes refuse to stay open. After more than thirty hours without sleep, I can hardly move.

"We'll stop at one of the stores so you can buy what you need." Emily turns to her husband and tells him where to go.

"I can't go shopping now," I mumble to Pablo.

"We don't have a choice," he mumbles back.

Couldn't we go to a hotel for one night and wait until tomorrow to go shopping? This sentence is ready to come out of my mouth, but I don't say it. These people seem to have gone to a lot of trouble to organize our stay, so I keep quiet.

Emily gets out of the car in front of a big store. She assures us we can find almost everything right there.

Mr. Grand goes across the street for a cup of coffee and asks us not to take long.

Emily walks from one end of the store to the other picking up all kinds of things she thinks we need and puts everything inside a cart she grabbed when we came in. I want to sleep. I'm sure my burning skin is bleeding. I don't care if we don't have sheets or towels or whatever. We can do this tomorrow. How much is all this going to cost? Doesn't she know we have a very limited budget? These thoughts ramble inside my mind but don't materialize into coherent ideas.

Pablo seems to be in a daze. He doesn't say anything. We walk behind Emily. I know I'm going to collapse at any moment. She keeps on rushing and saying things I don't understand, even though now I can speak and understand more than when we first arrived.

"We have to go to another store. I can't find dishes and . . ." Emily goes on with a list I can't assimilate.

Pablo finally opens his mouth. "We can wait until tomorrow."

"Might as well get it over with," Emily says. "No point in postponing what we can do now."

My stomach doesn't feel right. Nothing feels right. Among all these feelings, I want to kick Emily to the moon. I know she is trying to help us, but doesn't she see how exhausted we are?

She drags us to a couple of more stores before we finally stop in front of a small old building, a few blocks from the University of Texas.

"This is your home for the next month and a half," says Mr. Grand and gets out to help unload the station wagon. "I hope you have a pleasant stay in Texas. I'll pick you up tomorrow about six in the evening. There will be a reception for the Fulbright students. Next time you travel, don't bring everything you and your neighbors own."

I want to leave all of it on the sidewalk, but Mr. and Mrs. Grand must feel sorry for us and help take the luggage upstairs to our apartment. He opens the door and, with a "See you tomorrow," leaves us at the entrance.

I don't look at the apartment, closing my eyes to any task in waiting. All I want is for someone to take charge, to offer me a cool drink, something to eat, a comfortable bed, a word of encouragement, and some sympathy.

CHAPTER X

INTOLERANCE TO HEAT runs in my family. My mother seemed to melt away when she was in a hot-weather area. I know she was happy and grateful to live in a city where fall weather greeted her all year. My sisters and I do the same when the climate reaches eighty degrees; only my brother seems to take heat with gusto. My sister Marta lived in Chicago for a time. In the middle of the winter, she slept with the window open and the heat off. I am not that bad but pretty close. *In few words*, I hate hot weather.

The good Lord has taken me to many hot places in the world, but living in one of those places where the sticky heat of a summer day embraces you with hot chains never, ever crossed my mind. When, as a new young bride, I left the coolness of the Andes Mountains for the unknown land of the north, I did not know this kind of heat could cover some parts of the land, temporarily or permanently. It wasn't ignorance then. I knew about seasons, but in my romantic mind, summers were perfect warm times to enjoy the beach and other outdoor activities, not saunas in disguise.

July 6

The apartment is old, not fancy, but a big improvement from our basement abode in Washington. Sleeping aboveground is nice. To see the sun coming through the window in the morning is good for the soul, even though this first morning in Austin it fails to awaken us until close to noon when I reluctantly open my eyes and assess another dwelling. I think about the coming weeks. What awaits us in this big state?

I've never been so tired in my whole life. I ease myself up against the wall—there is no headboard. "Food! We didn't think about food. What are we going to eat for breakfast?"

Pablo is already out of bed. "I'm surprised Emily didn't take us grocery shopping yesterday."

"She probably had it on her list but we were out of time." I barely remember saying good-bye to the Grands. All I recall is rushing to the bedroom, spreading a sheet over the mattress, putting pillowcases on the pillows, and crashing.

I get out of bed. My spirit is up, but my body is feeling the abuse of the long trip. My raw skin still bothers me. Actually, I hurt all over. I need a good shower. I rush to indulge myself under the splash of reinvigorating water.

We are soon ready to explore our new surroundings. We walk around the luggage that fills most of the front room. Unpacking will have to wait. We close the door and leave.

Trying not to pay attention to the heat embracing us like fire, we walk a couple of blocks, guided by that inner antenna that works half the time; the other half, it makes fun of us.

"I can see the university over there." Pablo holds me by the hand and pulls me toward where he wants to go.

"First things first. We need to eat. It's too late for breakfast, so we have to make it lunch. I see movement over there." I point to a street a block away.

There are shops and businesses on Guadalupe Street. We go inside the first restaurant we see. I don't care if it is good or not. I just want to eat something and get out of the heat.

We order barbecue sandwiches. I hear that in Texas, barbecue is a must. The food is actually delicious. I want to order another sandwich, but we have to be careful with our money. Eating out is for special occasions or when we have no choice, like today.

With full stomachs we head for the campus. Pablo seems excited. For him, universities are heaven on earth. We stroll through the pathways where thousands of students have traveled on foot and on bikes for decades. Heat begins to melt me. I feel beads of perspiration forming on my face and neck.

"Let's go inside that building for a few minutes. I need to cool off." I don't wait for an answer and run to the closest building.

We visit a couple of places at the university and head for a small grocery store a student graciously walks us to. We buy bread, milk, eggs, and a few other items we need. The idea of having to cook in this weather is unimaginable. There are two window air conditioners in the apartment, one in the bedroom and one in the main room, but I don't remember seeing one in the kitchen.

July 8

It has been a couple of days since we first arrived in what seems like the hottest place on earth. Mr. Grand is in charge of the summer activities. Pablo is at the university during the day while I stay home unpacking what we need for our Texas stay and getting acquainted with the *American way of life*. At an orientation meeting the first night, we met with students from all of Latin America. Tonight we are going to a dinner, and this weekend we'll have a picnic by one of the lakes. It should be nice. Pablo is coming early from the university. We're going downtown to shop for summer clothes, like shorts and T-shirts, items we do not possess.

I make a couple of sandwiches for lunch, and soon we are on our way.

"Why are you walking so slowly?" Pablo stops and waits for me.

"I can't breathe in this heat," I say, dragging my feet.

It's too hot for humans. How did people ever colonize this land? They must have been different beings. My heart is full of admiration for the first pilgrims who came to this area and worked the fields, preparing the land for generations to come.

We have walked less than two blocks, and if I don't cool off, I know I will have a heat stroke. My mind wanders to the city where I was born, up on the Andes Mountains, where the temperature doesn't go over sixty-five to sixty-eight degrees. I close my eyes and force my imagination to bring upon me that delicious cool air that at times turns cold. I can almost feel it, embracing me lovingly. This feeling lasts but a second.

We walk in and out of stores to look for bargains, but mainly to get the benefit of air-conditioning. I can't walk one block without going inside a store. I hope I get over this, or I'm going to be very unhappy this summer.

We go into a small cafe, too tired from the heat to even talk. I'm sure our blood is not quite ready for this climate. It's either too thick or too thin. With faces dripping and dull brains, we sit with our heads down as I ask myself if we could become heat—exhausted.

"I thought I was tough and could take the heat, but it's getting to me." Pablo wraps his hands around a cold glass of Coke. "Did you get everything you need?"

"These two pairs of shorts and three T-shirts will have to do for now." I place the bags by my chair and slide the soft drink in my hand over my forehead. It feels good.

After a few minutes Pablo gets up and grabs the bags. "We better go back home now. We have to be at the International House before six this evening. A bus will take us to tonight's event."

We are ready to walk inside a huge restaurant, along with about fifty students. I like the plants surrounding the place and the spaciousness of it. This is something that has impressed me since we arrived here, the bigness of it all. Everything is Texas sized.

"Welcome to America. We are glad you are visiting our country." A white-haired man with a proud look addresses the audience in accented Spanish. "Some of you might not have ever been to a restaurant like this one."

I don't like his condescending tone of voice. I'm getting used to the United States being referred to as America, but does he really think we have never been to a restaurant? Perhaps I'm overreacting. Pablo looks at me with that look I know well, the one he wears when something or someone annoys him.

The white-haired man goes on and on about the American way of life. I tune out and concentrate on the crisp-looking salad in front of me.

"Hi, my name is Jorge, from Chile," says the man sitting by me.

I turn to him. "Hi."

He smiles. "This is my wife, Teresa." The smiling couple extends their hands to me and then to Pablo.

We talk about our countries and our families over a dinner of chicken, mashed potatoes, and vegetables—this seems to be the standard menu for these occasions—plus a delicious apple pie. We are told you cannot get any more American than this. The term *American* is becoming part of my vocabulary.

The day ends well, and I am pleased to have met the couple from Chile. We say good-bye to them as we get off the bus at the International House. We walk briskly toward our new home. Our new friends walk behind us. We wait for them.

"Where do you live?" I ask.

"A couple of blocks from here," Teresa says, catching up.

We continue talking until we reach our building. "We'll see you Saturday at the picnic," Pablo and I say at the same time.

"But . . . We live here too." Jorge laughs as he shows us the apartment next to ours.

"What a coincidence. So we are neighbors. It's going to be fun," I say.

"See you tomorrow," we all yell and go inside our respective apartments.

It's a good feeling to know that the people living next door to us speak our own language and share our culture. The world *culture* didn't mean much to me before. As I ponder about it, I can see that, even within my own country, there are several cultures since each region has its own customs. Now I am aware of many cultures. As fascinating as it is to learn about how people live in all corners of the world, it is very comforting to identify with people closer to your own way of life.

CHAPTER XI

*H*OMESICKNESS, LIKE A *brooding animal, attached its paws to my soul off and on for many years. This word doesn't encompass the immensity of what it means to describe. When homeland, family, and friends, so rooted in the innermost folds of a person's being, are stripped away, there is a feeling of profound loss, of not belonging. This feeling has become part of me. I even established—in my mind, and have written articles about it—a third culture, made up of those who live in a country other than their own. It is a good alternative. The knowledge that there are others in the same situation as mine gives me some sense of belonging, so important to one's sanity.*

Most third culture people agree that after more than ten years away from home, you don't seem to belong anywhere. You love your country, but you don't feel quite right in its entrails anymore, nor do you feel completely at home in the country where you live. There is a sense of "something different about me" wherever you go.

A song, the view of the countryside that takes me back to what I knew, a flower, or a special food can trigger a three-day homesick episode, tears galore, and that pain in the heart no aspirin can alleviate.

I have found solace and enjoyment in the country that has been my home for many years. We made peace with each other, and sometimes it makes me feel that we really belong together. But there is always that other country in South America that calls to me and asks me not to forget it. In a way I am lucky to have two home countries.

July 13

Last night it was horribly hot, and I couldn't sleep. It is early morning. Pablo is asleep, but I can't stay in bed any longer. I sit for a long time in the living room, the only cool place in the house. I recall memories of events and moments that seem to be in a world I don't want to let go. I close my eyes and again let the images of my recent life flow.

"What are you doing here?"

The voice enters my fuzzy brain. "I must have gone to sleep. It's too hot in the bedroom. I don't think the air-conditioning is working right. Can we get a fan or something? We don't want to bring the bed over here, right?"

Pablo looks at me as if I have gone mad. "It isn't that bad. I can sleep okay."

"My thermostat is different from yours."

"Okay. Let's have breakfast and then go get your fan. Do you realize this new item will have to be added to the luggage?" Pablo makes a face, showing his displeasure at the idea of carrying more stuff to our final destination.

"I can always sleep here, in front of this window air conditioner, if you think we shouldn't buy a fan."

"Is this what you want?" He looks hurt.

"Don't take it personally. It has to do with the heat and not with you."

I don't know why such a silly thing put a damper on the moment. Pablo is so sensitive sometimes. I go to the kitchen and serve two bowls of cereal. I'm getting used to eating corn flakes with milk mainly because it's so easy to prepare. I'm all for easy. Pablo pours two glasses of orange juice. We sit and eat in silence.

We get ready, and still in a huff, we go out searching for a fan. We don't have far to go. The drugstore, two blocks away, carries them. We go back home and wait for a sunnier moment while we try to look busy.

A feeling of loneliness overwhelms me. Since the first few days in Washington, when I sat and listened to the radio and cried for hours, I haven't felt like this. I go to the bedroom and turn on the radio. I switch from station to station until I find the romantic music that I know is going to make me cry. My thoughts backtrack through time with more intensity: Sunday dinner with my family, Christmastime at the ranch, my wedding day. The scenes rush through my head, making my heart ache. Tears pour down my cheeks faster than I can wipe them away.

Pablo comes in. He doesn't say anything. He puts his arms around me and kisses me.

"Are you hungry? Let's have soup and sandwiches and then go have ice cream. I'm sorry. I didn't mean—"

"Let's go." I interrupt him and run to the bathroom to splash water on my face. My eyes are swollen; I look terrible. I will try not to let homesickness get the best of me again, I promise myself.

The ice cream is delicious. I slide my tongue up and down my favorite Jamoca-almond-fudge cone. I want it to last for as long as possible. I have to accept that I am a chocoholic.

Pablo laughs at my exuberant reaction. He's a strawberry kind of person. I can tell we are not very adventurous as ice cream goes. We always order the same flavors.

"Do you want to go anywhere?" Pablo asks softly. "We don't have any planned program for today."

"It's too hot to walk or do anything, and it looks like it's going to rain. I'd rather go home."

We are back at the apartment and don't know what to do with ourselves. I go to the kitchen and wash a couple of dishes. Pablo grabs a book and thumbs through the pages. I can hear the rain hitting the windows. The front door bell rings, startling me. Who could possibly be calling?

"Hi. Have you ever seen anything like it?" asks Teresa, our Chilean neighbor.

"Seen what? Did anything happen?" A feeling of anxiety rushes through me.

"Look! LOOK OUT THERE. THE RAIN!" Teresa, followed by her husband, pulls me toward the window.

Pablo jumps out of his seat.

"I don't see anything." I look for a wreck or some dramatic happening out in the street. "What is it?"

"What about the rain?" Pablo asks, inching his face to the window.

"What about it?" I keep my eyes on the street, expecting to see a flood or something the rain could have done. It was raining hard but nothing to worry about.

"Have you ever seen rain like this?" Teresa looks at both of us as if we were not normal.

"Of course we have. This is nothing compared to the downpours in our country." I can't imagine why our neighbors are so surprised at the rain.

"It doesn't rain like this in Chile." Jorge, mesmerized, continues looking out the window as he talks. "It's fascinating."

We let them enjoy the rain, which doesn't last long. When it stops, I can't help laughing at such an idiotic happening. Soon we are all laughing. It's so interesting to find out that what we take for granted others find almost miraculous. The more I see and learn about the world and its people, the more I want to know.

We invite Jorge and Teresa to spend the afternoon with us. I can't wait to hear more about their country. It's strange to know that the four of us come from South America, speak the same language, and yet have such different experiences. As we go on talking, we come to the conclusion that we have a lot in common after all.

"Let's have dinner together." The words come out of my mouth without my permission. As soon as I say them, I go into panic. I can only cook a couple of things, and I don't have much food in the house.

"Great!" says Teresa. "I made a chicken casserole last night and still have half of it. I'll go get it." She acts on her words before I even open my mouth.

"I can put together a salad," I mumble, leaving Pablo and Jorge talking about mountains.

I'm glad I bought lettuce and tomatoes for sandwiches. I have become an expert sandwich maker since I can pile up lunch between two slices of bread. These "Americans" are pretty clever at inventing easy meals. I prepare a salad and send Pablo to get dressing and rolls.

We are having such a great time I don't want the evening to end. Teresa's casserole is wonderful. I wish I could prepare something so delicious. Perhaps one day . . .

"Let's do dinner again. Next time we'll do it at our apartment." Jorge, reluctantly, stands to leave. "See you tomorrow."

Teresa grabs her casserole dish, gives me a big smile and a kiss on the cheek, and leaves. I guess she is just as happy as we are to have found each other. I am beginning to look at friendship in a different light. I don't think I'll take it for granted again.

We pick up dishes and glasses and deposit them in the sink, too tired to do anything else. It's almost midnight when we go to bed. I carry the joy of friendship and sharing, along with the new fan, to the bedroom. I set the fan in front of my side of the bed and look forward to a cool and happy sleep.

CHAPTER XII

BEING AFRAID IS a feeling that afflicts most of the human race carries. We are afraid of those we perceive want to hurt us. We are also afraid of the environment that is poisoning us, of the traffic that stops us from moving, and of all the unimaginables out there.

It was not always that way for me. Even in my country—now widely known throughout the world for its violence—being afraid did not interfere with daily life. Walking in the streets of the city was not considered dangerous, even though meeting a thief was not out of the question; but thieves—usually—did not hurt you. They just snatched your purse and ran. Here in the United States it was even safer. In many towns, people did not lock their doors.

It doesn't seem possible that not so many years later, the world seems to be upside-down. We are now afraid of our own shadows. We bolt doors and install alarms in houses and cars, and surveillance cameras watch us everywhere. It's a miracle we all don't suffer from some kind of persecution complex.

I bring back the image of my very young self, walking the streets of Austin, oblivious to the world. At times I was afraid of people I didn't know because I didn't know what to expect. It was not in me then to see malice in those I met because I could not comprehend malice.

July 17

I can't wait to go to the lake. The little girl inside me is ready to enjoy a day in the country. In spite of the heat, I'm looking forward to this outing. I know it'll be different from what I know, but I can't wait to be part of a Texas barbecue.

I don't know what to wear to an occasion like this. I have come to the conclusion that everything I have is too formal. We might have carried pretty clothes from one side of the country to the other and ended up having no use for them. People here dress so informally. I have no idea what to wear. I don't think the comfortable clothes I bought the other day are pretty enough for this occasion.

"Pablo, do I look okay?" I'm wearing Bermuda shorts, a short-sleeved blouse, and a foolish look, I think.

"You always look pretty. But . . . this is kind of a different you."

"What do you mean by that?" I'm ready to go back and change into something that will make me feel more at ease.

"Don't be so sensitive. You look fine. I'm just not used to seeing you dress like this. Let's go. The bus will pick us up at the International House."

Pablo grabs his camera from the kitchen table. I throw my bag over my shoulder and rush out the door.

As we walk past the small grocery store, I remember we have no milk and bread. "I need to buy a couple of things. Do you think we can leave them at the International House until we return?"

"I don't see why not. There is a refrigerator over there. Why don't we buy them on our way back? I'd rather not carry packages."

"I don't know how late it'll be. I think they close early. There is nothing for breakfast tomorrow." I walk inside the store. Pablo follows me.

We arrive with enough time to put the bag of groceries in the refrigerator and get into the front seat of the bus. The morning heat is bearable, and the world looks bright.

"Teresa. Here. We are saving these seats for you!" I yell when I see our neighbor-friends climbing up the steps.

"Thank you. We are a little late. My parents called this morning from Santiago." Jorge smiles so big. It makes me envious.

I haven't talked to my parents since we left. In Washington it was difficult since we didn't have a telephone in the basement and did not want to bother Inéz and her husband. I sent Mama our number here in Austin. I hope they will call us. It's too expensive for us to call them.

After an hour's drive through the hill country, we arrive at a park by a beautiful lake. It's nice to see a few hills, no matter how low. I miss the mountains that embrace the city where I was born, the chain of mountains up and down the country, impressive, overpowering, beautiful.

After a delightful day of barbecue beef and chicken, potato salad and beans, boat rides and getting acquainted with people from all over Latin America, we're back at the International House. Texas is quite an interesting place. I can't figure out the people, though. They seem distant as if they didn't need anything or anybody outside their state.

It's a nice evening, and it's a little cooler. We are walking back to the apartment, along with Jorge and Teresa. The sun is beginning to escape the day, leaving us in the twilight.

"We forgot the groceries." The thought suddenly came to me.

We tell our friends to go on and retrace our steps back to the International House.

"I think I'll wait for you here by the gate while you go in." I don't know why I say that. I'm usually ready to go inside any air-conditioned place. It's warm but not too bad. I just don't want to move.

I lean against the wall, my eyes on the orange rays on the horizon. I feel lazy and can't wait to go home, sit back, and relax. After a day outdoors I need "indoor time."

The honking of a car's horn calls my attention. A man inside a big automobile seems to want to ask me something. He probably wants directions, but I won't be of any help. I barely know my immediate surroundings.

"Yes?" I ask and move toward the car.

He says something I don't understand.

"I'm sorry, I don't know what you are saying."

I hear him say "come," followed by a cascade of words that hit my ears without making any sense. I begin to feel uneasy, and I don't know why. He looks very businesslike since he is wearing a suit and tie. I can't figure out what he wants, so I decide to let him go find someone else.

I step back. "I don't speak English too well. I'm sorry but I can't help you."

THE OTHER AMERICA

The man moves toward the passenger seat and opens the door. Before I can react, he has taken hold of my arm and is trying to pull me inside the car. "What are you doing?" Fear clutches my throat.

"Come inside," he says, smiling. "I'll give you a ride to your place."

He speaks slowly and is close enough to me that I understand what he says. All the adrenaline inside me rushes through my body, and I scream the loudest scream ever to come out of my mouth. He pulls my arm. "Don't be afraid. Come inside."

"PABLO! PABLO!"

"MARCELA!"

I turn my face and see Pablo running toward me in panic.

I struggle to get loose from the stranger's grip. He suddenly lets go, and I fall backward on the sidewalk. I hear the screeching of tires and the roar of the engine as the car speeds away.

"What happened?" Pablo helps me up.

"That man, that man . . . He, he, he . . ." I can't talk.

"It's all right. Relax. You're okay now." I can see the anger on his face. "I wish I could . . ." He looks at the empty street as if he could will the stranger to justice.

We sit on the sidewalk for the longest time. I finally regain a little composure, enough to get up. My legs tremble. "I can't walk."

Pablo picks up the bag of groceries he had dropped. "We'll wait until you can."

He holds me for a while, and slowly we make our way back home. "Don't worry, everything will be okay."

We don't eat dinner. We don't talk about it. We quietly find refuge from the unknown in each other's arms.

I can't stop the tears and the sadness that cloud my soul. I know that trust in my fellow humans has gone out the window this evening. That man was not the poor, ignorant, petty thief I was used to seeing, but a well-to-do man I never expected to behave like that. My heart shrinks at the thought of what could have happened. Slow anger creeps inside me. I push it aside, pull my head up, and go on to bed.

CHAPTER XIII

MEETING NEW PEOPLE has always been difficult for me, a strange feeling for somebody who has lived in different countries and cultures.

A society standard is unique to a culture, with as many facets as people in it and a variety of backgrounds and social status. Back in South America, I was used to a formality of manners, dress, and behavior. In my social class there were rules and etiquette to follow and traditions to keep.

At first the "American" lack of social rules left me confused and sometimes unable to place myself. As time passed, I learned to enjoy the modus operandi of a society that invites friends to eat in the kitchen with the same ease and nonchalant attitude as they invite them to a most sophisticated dinner. The kitchen in this country is where everything happens, so why not invite friends over to share it with them? At the time I considered the kitchen a maid's domain. I still love to dress up for a formal occasion. I guess it's in my blood.

I've never forgotten the first time we stayed with a family we didn't know. I would have given anything to have been magically transported to the living room in my parents' house and never leave again. How grateful I am now for that wonderful family—our good friends—who made that adjustment easy.

July 30

For days I struggled with a fear that didn't want to leave until I decided to chase it with all my might. I can't let this incident pull me down. I'm sure to encounter situations like this along the way, so I better learn to deal with them, get tough, and take charge.

For the first time in my life, I'm holding a gun. I don't like it. Guns frighten me. However, Pablo is having a great time. He is like a little boy who has been given a yearning for this toy. The program for the day is taking place at a shooting gallery.

"Hold it steady and aim at the target," says the instructor, trying to keep my arm from shaking. "Now shoot."

I fire at the target in front of me. The tremendous noise and force throws me into panic as I feel myself fall backward.

I let go of the gun and manage to get up. Before the instructor can talk me into trying again, I'm out of there. I hate to behave like a sissy, but guns terrify me. It has amazed me to see rifles in the back of pickup trucks and holsters with pistols and revolvers hanging around the waists of Texas men. It brings the image of cowboys I've seen in the movies to a reality that in a way doesn't seem real.

The Texas experience has been quite unique. I'm sorry to see it end. It's hard to believe we have been here for almost a month. I'm still not used to the heat, but I'm weathering it somewhat better—I stay indoors as much as I can.

While I wait for the shooting session to end, I recall the interesting places we have been. This weekend we'll visit a host family in Houston and leave for Urbana, Illinois, next week.

August 10

Pablo stuffs his mouth with the last piece of toast on the table, drinks a glass of juice, and lets me know he's going to the university for an hour. He promises to be on time for our trip to Houston. We'll be traveling by car with Mr. Grand and another couple. We are all going to different cities in Texas.

Actually, I don't feel like getting ready yet. I'm sleepy and want to go back to bed. Last night we had dinner with Jorge and Teresa and talked half the night. I wash the dishes and walk back to the bedroom. I want to take a nap, but if I do, I will probably sleep for hours, so I turn around and head for the shower.

After a three-hour trip through the interesting Texas countryside, we reach Houston, and soon we stop in front of a very nice house in a wooded neighborhood.

A man with an infectious smile and a very pretty woman greet us and invite us to follow them inside. They introduce themselves as Fred and Mary Gray.

"I'll see you Sunday. I have to take the other couple to their family. Have a wonderful time," says Mr. Grand, leaving us with these strange people in a strange city.

"Let me take you to your room." Mrs. Gray ushers us out of a spacious family room to a very nice bedroom, decorated in an early-American fashion. "When you are ready, come and join us in the den. Take whatever time you need. I hope you enjoy your stay."

"Thank you, Mrs. Gray." I would give anything not to have to go through all of this. I push away my shyness and tell myself to act as an adult.

"Call me Mary. *Mrs. Gray* sounds so old." She smiles and leaves us.

It's great to be in a nice room again. It has been several months since we have slept in a real home, in a beautiful house. Being a student has a lot of drawbacks, I think, as I look around our accommodations for the weekend. I'm going to like it here.

Pablo sits in a chair in the corner. "Sometimes I feel as if I'm dreaming. We find ourselves in places we never expected. Host family. What a strange notion."

I agree with him. It almost feels as if we were living someone else's lives. It's eerie.

I take out a couple of dresses and a skirt and hang them in the closet. After a short rest, we head back to the family room.

Our host family is charming and makes us feel at home. We sit down with tall glasses of iced tea, the beverage we are still learning to drink.

Soon kids of all ages and sizes arrive from school. I can't memorize their names. The oldest, a girl just a little younger than me, comes in later in her own car. She's very pretty.

"Hi, I'm Robin. I can see you haven't done a lot of housework. Look at your hands and nails."

"I'm doing it now. A couple of more months and my hands won't look this way."

Mr. Gray takes us for a ride around the city. The neighborhoods we visit look wealthy. He tells us about the oil business and what it means to Texas as we drive by some oil wells. I remember seeing the strange-looking apparatuses along the road from Austin. I meant to ask Mr. Grand about them but got distracted.

"I hope you enjoyed your ride. Dinner is ready," says Mary, coming to greet us. Kids surround us.

It's wonderful to sit at a formal dining table for a change. I like informal sometimes, and I'm sure I'll be as informal as everyone else one day, but at the present, formal is my style.

Plates with the most appetizing foods sit in the middle of the table and are passed from person to person. The boys giggle. I'm sure they find our English pronunciation laughable.

"Tomorrow we'll be having lunch at the club, and in the evening we'll be going to church," Mary announces as we get ready to go to bed.

"That'll be nice. Thank you." The attention that the family we just met lavishes on us overwhelms me.

Why do these people take foreigners into their home? I ask myself, mystified by the whole affair. *Would I take strangers into mine?* I don't think I would. *Am I selfish or is this something that never entered my mind?* I can't answer this profound question. I better go to sleep. These deep thoughts are beginning to weigh on me.

August 11

After a most delightful day, we head for church. I'm uneasy about it. I've never been to a Protestant church. I don't know what to expect. I have ambivalent feelings. On one hand, I'm curious and can't wait to see what they do in a Protestant church, and on the other hand, I feel as if I'm betraying my beliefs. I can see in my mind my saintly grandmother's face, horrified at my going to any other church but a Catholic one.

I'm so disturbed I hardly know what goes on around me. There is a lot of singing and a long sermon I barely hear. People look nice and seem to pray with fervor. We all believe in the same God. I'm relieved when it's over. I don't understand my behavior. It's not as if I were doing anything wrong. I get close to Pablo. He smiles and puts his hand on my arm. He understands, making me feel better.

There have been too many new happenings to digest in such a short period of time. I again wonder about the many tomorrows ahead. A surge of energy suddenly takes over. I'll be ready to face whatever those tomorrows bring. *I know I will,* says my inner voice, a voice I hardly recognize.

CHAPTER XIV

THE MEANING OF the words discrimination *and* racism *were not part of my education until I came to the United States. I used to believe that I, my family, and people around me did not discriminate. How wrong can one be. In an unspoken code of behavior, those of us born to what was known as high society assumed that the lower classes were different from us.*

The discovery of my own prejudices descended on me in slow motion as I saw prejudice against blacks and people of other races in this other America. To learn that I considered those I perceived different because of their ancestry, ignorance, and station in life beneath me was a wrenching revelation. I still struggle with it. It isn't easy to overcome the pride of one's position, position not gained by any personal effort, attached to us with an invisible glue, so difficult to break that the world has been stuck to it in one way or another since the beginning of time.

August 29

Our good friends from Chile, along with Mr. Grand, have come to the bus station to see us off and help us with our huge luggage—another good-bye and another new place to adjust to. Will we ever see Jorge and Teresa again? Being at airports and bus stations and saying good-bye to new friends have become part of our life these days. I need to get used to it since we are going back to South America, and most likely we'll never see these people again.

"Don't forget to write to us." My heart aches as I embrace Teresa. "How are we going to get each other's addresses?" They are going to a university in Iowa in a couple of days.

"I'll send a letter to the International Center at the University of Illinois," says Jorge, waving as we climb the steps of another Greyhound bus.

With questions no one can answer, we settle in our seats, heading for the unknown. In about three months we have gone from South America to Washington, to Texas, and now to Illinois, a little too much for two young and inexperienced persons. Anxiety and insecurity creep in again, reaching my neck, strangling me. I breathe deeply. Shouldn't I be getting accustomed to hopping from place to place? But this time is different. We're going to our final destination, not to a month's orientation course. I had promised myself to face whatever came my way in an adult manner, and this I will do.

We sit in silence for a while. I stare at Pablo, curious about his thoughts. Are his concerns like mine? Knowing him, I could swear he's worrying about his courses. He's used to being the first in his class, receiving a laureate thesis for his six-year engineering degree and plenty of honors. He must be thinking about his academic performance in a language he hasn't mastered yet.

"I'm dreading another long trip." I interrupt the silence. "When we are through being students, I'll make sure we don't have to travel long distances by bus."

"I was just thinking about having to be inside this vehicle's entrails for two days. There is nothing to do but make the best of it."

After agreeing with him, we go back to silence. I hope I don't have to peel my skin from my clothing again. The idea of going through that little mishap was not appealing. I brought a small cushion with me. I trust it'll do the trick.

This time, not even the newness of the terrain around me makes me curious enough to alleviate the uneasiness I'm feeling. The first few hours are always the hardest because there are so many hours still to go.

We leave Texas behind. I don't have the map of the country clear enough in my head to know the states we go through. I'm getting hungry. We stopped only once, about three hours ago, not long enough to eat. The shadows of the evening are beginning to sneak across this part of the land. Soon it'll be dark.

The bus slows down. I welcome the stop since I am starving and moving around sounds great. I don't pay attention to the restaurant. Bus stops are pretty much the same.

"Let's get restrooms out of the way," I say, heading to where I see the signs.

"Where're you going?" The voice stops us.

"To the restroom," I mumble. I don't know what to think. A tall man, a passenger, stands in front of us, arms crossed, stern faced.

"Can't you read that it says, 'Colored people'? You aren't colored, are you?"

Colored people? What does he mean by colored people? Pablo and I look at each other in complete confusion.

"We have never been here," Pablo says in a low voice.

"Well, you can't go to those restrooms. Those are for colored folks. Restrooms for white folks are over there."

"Thank you," I mutter.

Pablo grabs my hand and pulls me in the other direction. "I didn't know there were separate restrooms for blacks. This is the South. I forgot about . . ." He goes mute as if he didn't know how to react to this unusual happening.

"We must pay more attention. That man was scary. I'll meet you in a bit inside the restaurant." I shake my concerns for the moment and walk inside the ladies' room for whites.

Now I'm aware of a situation I haven't noticed before. On the bus again, I see a few "colored people" in the back of the bus. Where did they eat? I didn't see them at the restaurant.

As we speed up the freeway, my mind crowds with images and preoccupations I didn't have until now. In Washington I was surprised at seeing black people because I was not used to them. Now I don't know what I feel. I don't want to deal with feelings I don't understand. Suddenly, my culture's own discrimination inadequacies appear as clear as a blue sky on a perfect day.

Pablo puts down the magazine he has been reading. "Why are you so quiet? You haven't said much in a couple of hours."

"I'm perturbed by this 'colored people' situation. It has made me think. So many people in the world were born in such a disadvantaged position, while others . . ." I can't think of anything else to say. The realization of the injustices in the world descends on me with incredible force. Life is unfair and difficult to understand.

We talk about it for a long time. This particular situation is new to us, so we don't know the depth of it, but we talk about it anyway. Pablo tells me of riots and slavery, which I know only enough to be aware of its existence. The two of us can go on for hours about these philosophical discussions. Somehow we have come to believe that, by talking about important issues in some way, we can make a difference. Humans can rationalize anything.

"What happened?" Pablo asks, awakening me.

It's pitch-black. "What?" I must have dozed off. The bus has stopped.

"We're going to be here for an hour or so," announces the driver.

People mumble and complain. "It's two in the morning," someone says.

The man who talked to us about "colored people" walks past us. I look the other way. We get off and enter a bus station. A few passengers walk to a counter to buy refreshments. I'm not hungry or thirsty. I just want a bed so I can sleep.

An hour goes by. I'm still sitting in the same seat. Pablo paces the station. No one seems to know what's going on. For some reason I feel kind of numb. It's raining outside. Somebody says something over the intercom, but I can't make it out.

Pablo rushes to me. "I heard we're going to stay here for a while longer, something about waiting for another bus. I'm going to ask. How can they keep us here like this?" He goes looking for someone with an answer.

Time goes by. I can see a dim light on the horizon. Soon it will be morning. Pablo doesn't find answers. His disposition deteriorates, and he continues pacing. We wait and wait until I begin to think we will never leave this dreadful station.

After hours of waiting we finally board the bus. We'll probably never know why we were detained at such an ungodly hour for so long.

August 30

It's early afternoon when we pull into the Greyhound station in Urbana. It feels like a carbon copy of the day we arrived in Austin, tired to the extent of feeling sick. We gather our huge cargo and stand by the curb.

"What now?" I ask. "Shouldn't somebody be waiting for us?"

"I thought so. Mr. Grand told me he would arrange for someone to meet us." Pablo looks around with a blank face.

We wait for a long time. I don't think I can keep my wits any longer. My body refuses to continue functioning. It needs rest, sleep, and care. I sit on a suitcase.

We wait for a long time. I'm afraid no one is coming to get us, but we decide to wait another half an hour before we worry. Besides, we have no energy to panic.

I can't think or do anything else but stare into space. It has been enlightening to find out that exhaustion sends my brain into hibernation. The world may collapse in front of me, and I won't notice.

CHAPTER XV

*T*HE IDEA OF *not having a nice place to live would not have ever entered my mind, much less having no place at all. While Pablo was a student, which covered a great chunk of time since he is a professional student, we lived in some abodes that were not what my heart desired.*

Finding myself stranded in a foreign country could not possibly happen to me, to us. To a newlywed couple, the first dwelling where they begin their life together is not only special, it's almost sacred. I knew that at first it had to be small and not pretentious; but a corner in a university building or the street was not part of my dream. It almost happened to us.

I don't know whether to laugh or to cry when I go back in time and see ourselves as the most inexperienced and naive couple in the world, so exhausted we could hardly move, dragging our feet along the streets of Urbana, Illinois.

August 30

I don't know how long we have been waiting. I don't feel my body anymore. Am I asleep? My eyes are open, but I don't really see what goes on about me. I shake my head to energize my brain. Do I have a weak body? According to Mama, I was a frail child. Do other people get this tired?

I was about to give up on whoever was to meet us when a young man, about Pablo's age, still panting from running, approaches us. "Hi. Are you Mr. Almán?"

Pablo nods.

"I'm sorry to be late. I didn't expect your bus to be delayed this long. I had to go do another errand."

"I'm glad you are here. Didn't they let you know when the bus was coming?" Pablo's voice has a slight reproachful tone. Someone has to get the blame for our fatigue and weariness.

"I'm Rod, a student at the university. I will take you to wherever you're staying." He doesn't address Pablo's complaint.

"We don't have a place yet," says Pablo.

"You didn't apply for housing?"

"I didn't know I was . . . I thought . . ."

Did we assume that it was somebody else's job to have a place ready for us? The Fulbright Program did it in Washington—even though we decided to use other accommodations—and also in Austin.

Rod looks at us and shakes his head. He lets us know there isn't anything available this late, that it'll be a miracle if we find a place to live. He'll take us to Housing at the university in the hope they might help us or store our luggage until we find an apartment.

Pablo thanks him, takes a couple of suitcases, and starts packing a big old car.

By the time we finish, the clunker seems to be flat on the ground.

"I think we're going to have to make two trips. There is no way I can make this old thing move with all that weight." Rod takes a few bags out of the backseat.

Pablo, looking distressed, stays behind with half the load.

I jump in the passenger's seat. I let Rod do the talking, too tired to say anymore than answer his questions. Whatever good information he is giving me is not registering. We stop in front of a low building inside the university campus.

"Wait here while I ask someone about a place to leave your stuff."

This luggage has given us so much trouble I want to dump everything in the nearest trash bin. I'm glad the weather is cooler in this part of the country. I couldn't have waited inside a car in Austin. What are we going to do if we can't find a place to live? All kinds of thoughts assault my mind, but I'm too exhausted to work myself into one of my panic fits.

"It took me some doing to convince them, but you can leave your things here for a couple of days."

Rod takes the bags someplace inside and leaves me at the entrance of the Housing Office, wishes me good luck, and goes back to the station to pick up my husband and the rest of our belongings.

How am I going to communicate well enough with these people to try to talk them into helping us? I see a nice-looking man sitting behind a counter.

Finding hidden energy somewhere inside my tired body, I explain our situation the best I can. It takes a lot of repetition before he grasps the meaning of our predicament.

"I can't believe you come here, a few days before classes begin, without housing arrangements. Everything is taken. I am sorry."

The man tells me we should have applied for graduate housing, that all he can do is to help us keep the luggage until we find a dwelling. He advises us to go buy a newspaper at a drugstore and look in the classified ads for a place close to the university. I think that is what he said.

I want to cry, but I can't and won't. I go out to the hallway to wait for Pablo.

Rod and Pablo unpack the car. Rod takes the rest of the luggage to join the other suitcases and takes us to a drugstore, smiles, waves, and disappears.

We go through the rental ads. There is no way for us to know if these properties are close to the university. We decide to circle the ones with the best prices and ask the person at the store where we bought the newspaper.

He tells us there is one close-by. We walk several blocks to an old house and ring the bell. A middle-aged woman with bleached hair opens the door.

Pablo steps up to her. "We are here about the apartment you have for rent."

"It's rented already. Sorry. There are a couple of apartments not far from here. They may have something." The woman bows and dismisses us.

We walk block after block until I feel I can't put one foot in front of the other anymore.

THE OTHER AMERICA

"Let's call some of these numbers in the newspaper," I say, not willing or able to continue scrambling from one end to the other of a town we don't know, to find that the place is not available any longer.

We go back to the drugstore and call from there. We get the same response from every rental in our list. "Sorry, it's already rented" is the standard answer.

"What are we going to do?" I ask, knowing there isn't an answer. I can't walk anymore. I sit on the sidewalk. Pablo joins me.

What a pitiful sight we must be. My numb brain doesn't send any messages. With our elbows resting on our knees, we hold our heads for a time. I don't know if it's a long time. I don't seem to have a sense of reality. How could we be sitting on a sidewalk in a town where we don't know a soul? There is not even a Mr. Grand here.

"Let's go back to the Housing Department. They should be able to help us somehow until we find a place." Pablo stands up and extends his hand to me, pulling me to my feet.

I don't answer. I drag my feet as I try to follow Pablo. I can see us sleeping on top of the suitcases in a corner of the Housing Department building. How could this be happening to us? I wish we weren't so tired.

We arrive a few minutes before closing. The nice man is arranging papers, ready to leave. "Did you find an apartment?"

I shake my head, tears ready to bathe my face.

"Everything is taken. It's late and we need a place to stay. Could you help us?" Pablo uses his most convincing voice.

I know I have to get hold of myself, be strong, and act. I'm good at talking people into helping. But what can I say in a foreign language? We're at such a disadvantage.

"Please, help us. There must be one of the graduate apartments available. Could you please check? We don't know anyone here. If you don't help us, we'll have to sit here day and night because we can't live in the street. You have to find something for us." These are the words I think I'm saying, but I can tell by the man's expression that I must be using wrong tenses and words that do not mean what I want to say. I stop talking, unable to hold back the avalanche of tears. Being strong is not so easy, especially when exhaustion threatens to make a dunce out of me.

I try, but I can't stop crying. Someone brings me a glass of water. Pablo tells me to calm down, that everything will be okay, but I keep on bawling until I empty my soul of fear and frustration through cleansing tears.

"Now, now, you sit here while I check and see if there is something I can do." The nice man pats me on the back and goes to his desk.

We sit and wait. I sigh. Did the man give us his name? If he did, I don't remember it. He looks at papers and folders for the longest time. On pins and needles, Pablo and I look at each other and continue waiting.

"Well. This is your lucky day." The man finally looks up. "I see here that someone canceled today. There is a one-room apartment available. Let me call the manager of that particular building. It's furnished, so you can move tonight. I don't know if it has been cleaned."

"It's okay. We'll clean it." Pablo gets up and extends his hand to the man. "Thank you. We appreciate what you have done for us."

"Thank you," I say between sighs.

We walk out of the building with tired bodies, blisters on our feet, and hope in our hearts and more than ready to go to our first real home, prepared to take on the next stage awaiting us, once we had a good night's sleep.

CHAPTER XVI

*B*EING THE LADY *of the house has always sounded strange to me. It has a connotation of housewife—cleaning, cooking, and other similar tasks. The man of the house means the man in charge, the one who owns the place. I don't know if this is the way other women perceive these two words, but this is how I understand them. The term makes me uncomfortable.*

I love to have the house to myself during the day, so seeing it from this perspective, I am the lady of the house. I arrange and rearrange furniture and decorations for months until it pleases my senses. I'm uneasy and unhappy when I'm surrounded by clutter or the wrong decor. This is something that runs in my family. We go to great lengths to decorate our habitats with a personal touch.

Decorating an apartment furnished with the bare necessities and having no extra money to spare on such frivolous matters as decorations have been a challenge at times. Along the way I have been faced with this predicament, but none was as difficult as that first dwelling in Urbana.

August 30

I have arranged and rearranged in my mind our first home many times. I never expected it to be so far away that we couldn't get our own furnishings to make the place the home of my dreams. That home will have to wait. Meanwhile I'll have to make do.

The apartment manager takes us to the fifth floor of a building, one of four forming a square. He says something about the refrigerator, keeping the place in good order, and something else I hardly hear. Then he gives us the key and leaves. The sun is beginning its daily descent.

Pablo unpacks the sheets and pillows we bought in Austin. He pulls out the sofa bed and spreads the sheet. "I'm going to take a shower."

I take off my shoes and stretch out on the mattress. "Hurry, I also want to take one."

There is only one room with a green sofa bed. At the other end of the room there is a small table and two chairs, a kitchen, and a bathroom somewhere. I'm too tired to look. I close my eyes while I wait for Pablo to come out of the bathroom. We need something to eat, but I can't face that task now. I can feel myself going into a kind of slumber.

August 31

Where . . . ? What time . . . ? I sit up. A bright sun announces a new day. Is it really morning? It must be. It was not quite dark when I closed my eyes. I know the sun was not shining this way. How long have I been asleep? I'm still wearing the clothes I had on yesterday. Pablo's back is turned toward me. I quietly slip out of bed and walk to the kitchen in my bare, sore feet. It's small, with a stove, a refrigerator, and a few cabinets. I move to the window behind the table. I see a nice grass-covered area and a few trees. It looks like a small park fenced in by the buildings.

"Hi. Did you sleep? You were dead to the world last night." Pablo puts his arms around me. "I heard you get up. These long bus trips have to end. I feel as if I've carried the bus on my back instead of the bus carrying me."

I laugh. We savor the moment and stare out the window.

Pablo sits in one of the chairs and tells me we are down to about ten dollars and we need to buy food.

I sit in the other chair. "We'll just have to find foods that go a long way, like cereal, beans, rice, pasta . . . When will you get your first monthly check?"

"We have to make do the best we can this weekend. Today is Saturday. There is nothing I can do until Monday. We need to pay the rent within the next five days, so I hope the money comes soon."

I chase away the worry threatening to spoil the first day in our new home. I take a shower, and soon we are on our way to buy food.

A woman comes in the building as we open the glass door to go out.

I ask her about a grocery store in the area. I speak slowly so she can understand me. I tend to talk fast, and somehow I want to transfer the speed to a language I barely know, which doesn't help.

"There is a small one across that street." She points to the right.

She introduces herself, but I can't understand her name. I thank her for the information, smile, and head for the food. I'm starving. I don't remember what we ate yesterday or if we ate at all.

I'm glad we have a store just across the street. It's small but nice. We carefully choose items that I believe will give us the most servings for the money. I think about my parents and how worried they were about us not having enough funds to live on. In the last letter I received, Mama said they had tried calling us in Austin but could not make the connection.

We buy two cans of tomato soup (the least expensive of canned soups), two cans of pork and beans, a two-pound rice bag, a box of cereal, milk, bread, luncheon meat . . .

Back at the apartment I clean the cabinets and put the groceries away. I forgot to get cleansers, and I realize the list is endless and we don't have enough money.

Pablo is arranging the suitcases against the wall. "Which one should I open first?"

Before we left Austin I remember packing sponges, dishwasher soap, and a couple of cans of something. "This one has what we need now. Let's eat and then we'll get busy."

My stomach seems to be getting accustomed to canned food if I don't eat it every day. I don't really care for it, but it is cheaper than fresh food. For the time being I'll endure it.

While we eat cereal, Pablo, with a worried look, clears his throat. "This apartment is more expensive than we can afford. After we pay rent and utilities, we don't have much left for anything."

In our haste to get the apartment we did not stop to consider the price, too frazzled to think about money. I believed university housing for graduate students should be within our budget.

"We're going to have to eat tomato soup, pork and beans, and rice until you graduate. My stomach isn't going to like it, but there is not much we can do."

Pablo smiles but doesn't say anything.

I look around the bare apartment: no pictures, no curtains, nothing to make it look like a home. I'm going to have to be creative since having food to eat comes first.

"Let's don't worry about money." Pablo puts his hand on mine. "I want to go see the campus. I believe it's as big as the University of Texas campus. We'll unpack later."

Talking about money is something Pablo would rather *not do*. Telling me there was only ten dollars left must have been quite disagreeable to him. His family is one of those families that consider money matters dirty talking.

He puts me in charge of finances. He says I'm a lot better with money than he is. He thinks I am a good manager. I believe he is right.

I get up and take my bowl to the kitchen. It's a good idea to get acquainted with the university and surroundings. Since I'm going to be taking English classes, I also need to know where to go.

Pablo brings the rest of the dishes and goes to turn the bed into a couch for the day. We can just get up and go, but I can't stand to come back to an untidy house, so I unpack the sponges and go to the kitchen to do what I never imagined doing—*housework*. In Austin and in Washington it was difficult, but it seemed to be a game, like when, as a little girl, I played house. It now seems like serious business, one I have to learn to endure.

The weather is nice, warm, but so much cooler than in Texas. It's almost September, and fall should be in the air soon. I like the idea of seasons. I was used to a city with the greatest weather in the world, but it is pretty much the same all the time. I look forward to seeing snow. Snow-covered fields look so beautiful in the movies. I can't wait to feel the white flakes falling on me.

I'm not up to a lot of walking; we did enough of it yesterday, so we stroll along trails and paths. Pablo's face lightens when he sees the engineering building where he'll be taking most of his classes.

We decide to take it easy, go back to the apartment for lunch, and then take a nap. It's going to take the whole weekend to recover from the ordeal.

I want to unpack as soon as we get some rest, before Pablo gets too busy at the university. He lets me know classes won't start for a week, but he still has to talk to a lot of people, register, and get books and other items, so we'll have to unpack this weekend.

At the apartment Pablo opens a can of tomato soup and warms it while I make sandwiches. I'm now an expert on this kind of meal.

After lunch Pablo gets the bed ready for our siesta. He complains about having to pull out and push back the couch one or more times a day.

When I get back from the kitchen, he's already asleep. I stretch out on the bed and begin planning how to make the apartment a little more *me*.

I can use a cardboard box as a coffee table if I cover it with a small tablecloth. I packed a few wedding presents I can use to decorate the place. We have been living in temporary quarters for so long I'm eager to make this abode into a home.

The sound of ringing reaches my subconscious. I open my eyes. My whereabouts come slowly to my sleepy head. No one knows us here. Who could be calling? It must be the building manager.

"What is it?" Pablo sits on the bed.

I smooth my clothes, slip on my shoes, and rush to open the door.

"Hi, I'm Chris," says a very pretty Oriental young woman. "I know you just moved in. I saw you bringing your luggage inside. My husband and I live down the hall in 512. I know how it is when you come to a new place where you don't know anybody. Here, I cooked this for you."

What an unexpected happening. This woman, who has never seen us, cooked dinner for us? Unbelievable. "Thank you. It's so nice of you."

She hands me a casserole dish covered with foil. "I hope you like it. Let me know if you need anything. Bye now."

I'm speechless. "Can you imagine?" I turn to Pablo, who waits on the bed. I set the plate on the table. "There are some good people in the world," I say, ready to enjoy the fruits of someone else's labor.

Did Chris's food contain special power, or is it the fact that someone cares that is giving me inner strength? I feel like another person who can face most anything, not like the naive, pampered girl of a few months ago. I know I will be back to being that naive, frightened girl every so often, but it won't last, I hope.

CHAPTER XVII

*L**EARNING A FOREIGN language is an ordeal for anyone. Having to study for a graduate degree in a tongue other than your own is an incredible challenge. Remembering the difficulties we had the first year in the United States makes me wonder how we got to master the language well enough for me to write books, stories, and articles in Spanish and in English and for Pablo to obtain a couple of PhDs and to work and teach engineering classes in English.*

The misunderstandings and strange situations I found myself in while learning a language that tangled my tongue were embarrassing and sometimes funny for others, but not for me.

September 6

It's chilly. I button my jacket. I'm on my way to the University Health Center to have some tests run, required for enrollment, even though I'm only taking one class. Pablo's appointment is this afternoon. I wish his had come first.

I'm anxious about it. I don't know what to expect. I don't like going to the doctor. Almost every time I went to the doctor as a child, I got an injection. Since my asthma required weekly shots, I associated visiting a doctor with this kind of treatment.

Pablo began classes Tuesday, after Labor Day. We're both taking English for foreign students on Wednesday. My pronunciation is pretty awful. A French student in our first class argued forcefully about the pronunciation of the *h*. He doesn't agree and wants to change the language to what he considers correct. I predict he'll never learn.

Students run in all directions, carrying books and backpacks. Bicycles rush by me. A girl wearing glasses asks me directions to the mathematics building. "Sorry, I am new," I say and continue making my way to where I'm going. Yesterday we walked to the Health Center, so for a change, I know where to go.

I've been sitting in a waiting room for almost an hour when I hear someone calling, "Marcela."

A nurse, half-hidden behind a door, asks me to follow her.

Another nurse greets me with a dreaded thick needle she inserts in my right arm. I have good veins, but the woman takes forever to push the needle in all the way and draw blood. I bite my tongue and endure it.

The nurse directs me to the next place where I get my eyes checked. Like a zombie, I follow different nurses to cold, unwelcoming rooms where they poke me, take more tests, and look me over from head to toe.

A young nurse comes and asks me to do something I don't understand. She repeats the request several times, but I have no idea what she wants. I feel like an idiot, and the nurse is at a loss. The more I try, the more nervous I become and the less I understand.

"Stay here," says the young woman and disappears.

She returns and hands me a small plastic cup, takes me by the arm, and parks me in front of a bathroom. "Oh!" I say, feeling like the most stupid person on earth. I know I blush. I can feel it. I want to hide. I need to learn this language even if it kills me.

September 15

"You need to rest, Pablo. You can't stay up all night studying."

It's difficult for me to sleep with the light on, even if it's a lamp by the dining table. I worry about Pablo. He's able to go for hours without sleep, but for the last two weeks, he barely takes a snooze, and a couple of times I've heard the shower in the early morning, without him ever making it to bed. I'm not sleeping well, and he's not sleeping at all.

Pablo puts the book down. "If the professors were not writing most of what they teach on the board, I wouldn't know what they were doing. Reading is easier since I'm used to reading in English and I know the subject, but I need more practice so I can understand and get hold of this language or I'm not going to make it."

I sit at the table by him. "It takes time to learn a language. I thought we were doing well. We understand so much more now."

"It's not enough for my studies." Pablo's face hardens. "I can't wait until the semester is over and I have flunked every course. I don't do flunking. Not me. I need your help. It isn't going to be easy for either of us. Will you be willing to speak English all the time? It's the only way. You're good with languages, and it'll be great practice for both of us."

It's an interesting idea, and it makes sense. "It'll cut communication to a minimum. Fighting will be out. I don't think we can manage a good fight in English."

Pablo laughs. "That's a plus. After a while, when I feel I understand most everything, we can speak in Spanish after seven in the evening."

"You have it all arranged, huh? It isn't going to be fun, but we can try."

September 23

I was right. It is awful. We have been murdering the English language for over a week. The muscles in my mouth hurt. I'm sure the vowel sounds will probably damage my mouth muscles forever. An *a* doesn't always sound like an *a*. Sometimes it sounds like the *a* in Spanish, like in *cat*, but other times it's a completely different pronunciation. This happens with every single vowel. Maddening. I'm beginning to sound like the Frenchman in my class. Some days I foolishly believe I've gotten good at speaking in this strange lingo, only to find out the next day that I'm tongue-tied.

There is a doughnut shop across the street from our apartment building. I walked past it this morning and noticed a sign that read,

"Help wanted." We're so short of money that I'm considering this possibility.

I meant to go in but could not make myself do it. This is not something I would do in my country. I know it's different here. Most students do this kind of work but . . . me? I'll talk to Pablo tonight after seven. This isn't something we can discuss in English.

We're now beginning to apply the seven o'clock rule. It took more than a week before Pablo felt we could go back to our native mode of communication for a few hours. Some days I feel I can't speak in either language. My tongue is completely tangled.

"What do you know about doughnuts?" asks Pablo, looking at me as if I had gone crazy.

"Not much but it shouldn't be too difficult. We need some extra money. The scholarship barely pays the rent and utilities. Aren't you tired of tomato soup and pork and beans?"

"I don't like you doing this kind of work." He pauses. "This troubles me. I—"

"Don't fret. I'm sure we aren't the only couple facing money woes. As a foreign student—without a green card—I'm allowed to work a few hours a month. It shouldn't be too bad." My words are more optimistic than I really feel.

September 25

It's settled in spite of Pablo's qualms. I got the job. I begin today after lunch. I'll work three afternoons a week.

I don't want to be late, and yet I want to delay a task I never expected. The tough realities of life don't seem to be present in a young girl's dreams. I chase my misgivings away and step out the door. *You do what you have to do*, I tell myself as I rush to my new job.

A short man wearing an apron welcomes me. He shows me all kinds of doughnuts with different names. I get so confused. I want to forget the whole thing and run back home. I don't know what I'm doing here anyway. It takes everything I have to stay put and face a job I don't want to do.

A woman comes in and asks me for what I think is a sugar doughnut. It isn't. It takes three tries before I give her the strawberry jelly one she really wants.

People come in and out. They speak too fast for me to understand which kind of pastry they want. Most of the time I give them the wrong flavor, and the owner gives me reproachful looks. I decide not to look at him, concentrating on what I'm doing. Two students come in the middle of the afternoon. One of them, a chubby young man, takes pity on me and helps me when he sees me looking at the customer, completely lost. He points at what the client wants.

Before going home the owner gives me a pat on the back. "You're getting the knack of it. I'm sure you'll do well."

I can't believe it's time to leave. My head hurts. The idea of coming back the next day gives me a stomachache.

September 27

Between having to speak English all day and working at the doughnut shop, I feel again as if I were a stranger inside. There is no way it can be me.

I have worked three afternoons and don't seem to get any better at doing my job. If the nice chubby student doesn't work my hours, I give jelly doughnuts to those who ask for glazed and sugar to the customers who ask for plain. I rarely get one right. Is it nervousness? I understand most of what people say to me, so why don't I get what the clients ask for?

The owner calls me to the back room. "I'm sorry, Marcela, but you aren't working out. The customers are complaining. I can't afford to wait for you to understand what people want. I'm sorry. Here is your check."

I don't know whether to cry or to laugh. I take the check and leave. While I cross the street to go home, it dawns on me. I've been fired from my first job in this country after only a few days. I don't know what I'm going to do to make some extra money. But there is one thing I'm sure of: I don't ever want to see a doughnut again.

My bruised pride needs consolation. I ache to call my mother and let her heal my wounds. Being fired is a humiliating experience even when you don't want the job.

CHAPTER XVIII

*A*FTER STRUGGLING FOR *years and making several people sick in the process, including myself, as I have stated before, I finally learned how to cook. It is surprising my family lived through it.*

Since I expected to have a cook, my mind refused to do this task well, along with many other household chores I did grudgingly. I thought I didn't have to learn because the situation was temporary, and I would soon have that fantastic cook my mind had created. When we went back home for a time, we did have a cook, not exactly the perfect one I had in mind, but a cook nevertheless.

At first I tried to overcome my inadequacies in the kitchen, but my ignorance on the subject won over my good intentions.

September 28

I don't have a job but—in spite of my wounded ego—I feel pretty good. The fact that I'm not going back to the doughnut shop has taken the ache from my stomach. We humans are strange creatures, and at times we don't make sense—at least I don't.

With the money I earned yesterday, I went to the store on my way home and bought a box with the ingredients to make pizza. I also bought lettuce, tomatoes, peaches, eggs, and French bread. I feel a need to celebrate not that I was fired but at having a little extra money to indulge in a good dinner.

I've been busy all day, catching up with the tasks I didn't have time to do while working. I change the bedsheets, then go to the laundry room downstairs to do the wash, and back up again to straighten the apartment. Pablo is coming home early. On Saturdays he goes to the library to study.

I would love to sit at the table, set and ready for a great meal that I didn't have to cook. I know this won't happen for a while, so I better concentrate on this special dinner I'm fixing tonight.

I follow the direction on the box. For the preparation of the pizza, pour the sauce on top of the dough and put it inside the oven to bake. I set the table, make a salad, and cut the peaches for dessert.

"Hi! I finished studying earlier than expected. It smells so good. I'm starving." Pablo seems to be in a great mood.

"Today's dinner is a surprise. It should be ready in a few minutes."

"I'm so glad you're not working at the doughnut place. You're not upset they let you go, are you?"

"I was upset and yet happy. I did try though. I didn't like working there, so leaving freed me."

"Don't give it another thought. We won't talk about it anymore." He hugs me and sits down at the table. "I can't wait to eat your surprise."

I bring the salad and ask Pablo to get the pizza while I serve us something to drink. I divide a can of Coke in two glasses with lots of ice. We are set for our big dinner.

Pablo sets the pizza in the center of the table. "I've never seen a pizza look this way. It looks more like a cake."

"What on earth . . . ?" I can't believe what I see. It does look like a cake with red sauce on top. It's supposed to be flat. I followed directions. I don't understand.

"Well. It's still a pizza since it's made with the right ingredients. Might as well eat it." Pablo takes a knife and cuts a big piece for me and another for him.

What did I do wrong? How can pizza dough rise like this? What's done is done, so I grab my fork and proceed to enjoy my strange-looking piece of cooking art.

I don't say anything, but it tastes like it needed to be cooked longer, even though the outside is pretty crisp. It's somewhat rubbery inside. I spread the sauce throughout it, impregnating the inside dough with it. It isn't too bad. The salad is pretty good, so are the peaches. All in all it is a special dinner.

I stare out the window. I see a lot of people sitting on the grass, talking. I've seen them almost every day. "It's still daylight.

Why don't we go down to the courtyard? Look, our nice Japanese neighbor is talking to a man, probably her husband."

We have been so busy trying to survive we haven't had time to meet but a few people. Besides, we still feel inadequate about the language. The neighbors we have met coming in and out of the building seem very nice, giving us a warm welcome. Our next-door neighbor brought us a cake when we first moved in, and another brought cookies. We thanked them as we did Chris, but we have not seen them again. I never expected people to be so nice.

Pablo doesn't seem too excited about my plan, alleging the need to finish a project. I tell him he can't study day and night and that we need a little relaxation, so he agrees.

We go down and stroll around the courtyard, not knowing how to go about socializing with people we don't know. It's awkward since we have no idea how it's done here. We don't have an organization planning events for us or our Chilean friends coming to visit. I have missed Jorge and Teresa more than I imagined.

It's one of those perfect days, neither cold nor hot. "Indian summer at the end of September," I heard someone comment at the grocery store yesterday. I have no idea what it means, but I gather it's a warm day when it's supposed to be cool.

I sit against a tree trunk. Pablo does the same.

Chris walks toward us. I haven't seen her since I returned her casserole dish and thanked her again.

"Hi. I'm so glad you decided to come out. Let me introduce you to some of the neighbors."

Several men and women, who greet us warmly, soon surround us. Chris tells us she was born in Chicago from Japanese parents. She and her husband are students. I like them. They are a very good-looking couple, tall and handsome. It's pleasant to just sit and visit. It's good for the soul to pause and forget worries and duties for a little while.

"Come to my apartment for a drink," says a woman with long blond hair to Chris and her husband, two other couples, and us. "My husband is taking care of the kids. He'll be glad to get off the job."

We walk alongside the others as we silently ask what this encounter will bring.

"I'm Joanne," says the woman as we walk inside her apartment. "Please feel at home. I'll put drinks on the table. Help yourselves."

The room is so cluttered it's difficult to find a place to sit. There are toys everywhere, books, papers, and odds and ends. I moved a stuffed animal, and we both sit on the sofa.

As I walk to where Joanne had put several soft drinks and a few cans of beer, I look toward the kitchen. There are dirty plates, pots, and pans everywhere. In some way I envy people who are not bothered by the chaos around them. I have to have everything neat and organized, or the turmoil moves inside me and I can't function.

Joanne's husband is working on his PhD. He is Arab and a most interesting person. They have two boys, who come to meet us and then are taken to bed against their wishes. We can hear them cry for some time.

Tonight I feel I can understand almost everything, making the moment more meaningful. It's nice to finally meet people we can visit with sometimes. A feeling of warmth and acceptance purrs inside me. Since we left family and country, I have felt like I'm walking inside somebody's house without being invited.

After a couple of hours Pablo gets up. I follow him, thank our hosts, and leave. My stomach is queasy. The taste of pizza is still in my mouth. I take an antacid and go to bed.

Pablo takes his books to the dinner table to work on his project.

Nausea awakens me. As I sit up I feel my insides rising to my throat. I barely make it to the bathroom.

"Are you sick too?" Pablo asks as I come out, walking unsteadily.

"I feel awful. You feel bad too?"

"Yes. I've been throwing up for a couple of hours. What did you put in that pizza?" he teases.

"Whatever it was is making us very ill." I hate to feel sick to my stomach, especially since I was so sick in Washington. I sit down at the table and hold my head. I consider taking another antacid but decide against it since the idea of swallowing anything makes bile rush up my throat. It's going to be a miserable night and not a good day tomorrow.

Pablo gets up. "I can't concentrate. Let's try to get some sleep."

After emptying my stomach for the fourth time, I decide that from now on I'll let others do the pizza cooking. I go back to bed, wondering if I'll ever be one of those creative women who cook fabulous meals, have a spotless house, and look like a million dollars. I probably saw them in magazines. They can't possibly exist. I will settle for just palatable food that won't make us sick and work on the other qualities another time.

CHAPTER XIX

PEOPLE BUY THINGS they can't afford all the time. It's strange, but there is an optimistic feeling that somehow the money will automatically appear to pay for a purchase obtained by using credit when there are no available funds. Most of us go ahead and do it anyway.

Not many can say they have not owed or still owe hundreds and thousands of dollars, pounds, pesos, or whatever currency is used. I've never liked this mode of financing, but it has been hard to refute Pablo's philosophy of "We only have one life to live. If a person needs a car, furniture, a trip, or anything else, might as well do it now, because then it'll be too late."

In some way I know he is right, but at the same time, I hate to have debts. I worry about not having enough money to pay the bills. Peace of mind is my motto. At times I wanted to strangle Pablo for putting his philosophy into practice even though half the time his expenditures were presents for me. There were other times we had to buy what we needed, like a car, a refrigerator, or another expensive item that took months or years to pay since students are usually poor. Pablo loved studying and collecting degrees, keeping the student status longer than desirable.

October 13

I'm very careful with food these days, sticking to what I know, leaving adventurous cooking for later years when maturity and experience kicks in. It'll be boring for a while, but so far no one is complaining, at least not aloud.

"We can't go anywhere without a car. We're stuck here all the time," Pablo says as we finished breakfast Sunday morning, two weeks after the pizza fiasco.

"We can't afford to buy a car now. We barely have enough money to eat cheap food."

"We can buy a secondhand car on credit. The University Union lends students money to buy a car as long as the amount is reasonable. The monthly payment is very low."

The idea of another bill to pay makes me so nervous I can't breathe. "It's not that we have a lot of time or money to go places. You're always studying. You don't even have time to sleep."

He tries to convince me it won't cost much. One of his classmates knows a very good dealer, and he will take us there. Pablo looks at me like a little boy who asks his mother for a toy he wants badly.

He talks me into it, and few hours later we're on our way to the dealer. Pablo's friend seems nice. We don't talk much while he drives us. I keep on doing math in my head, and it doesn't add up. No matter how I stretch the numbers, the result is the same—eat or pay for a car.

It doesn't take long for the salesman to persuade Pablo of the absolutely incredible deal he is offering us: a seven-year-old gray Dodge. According to him, it had barely been driven outside the area. I stop listening and walk away.

A couple of hours later we say good-bye to Pablo's classmate and drive away in our new old car. It's nice to have wheels to go places but . . .

Pablo smiles widely and asks me where I want to go.

We have been living around the university since we arrived, so I have no idea what lies beyond it.

He keeps his eyes on the road and says, "Let's take a ride around the city and then stop for ice cream."

It's enjoyable to go to neighborhoods we had no idea existed. We stop at an ice cream shop and have my favorite, Jamoca almond fudge. Then we visit several stores and get lost for a long time before heading back home.

October 19

Saturday, after paying the bills, I let Pablo know we have to find a way to make extra money. We have five dollars left for food and a car payment to make.

"You're not thinking of going back to the doughnut shop, are you?" Pablo pours himself another bowl of soup.

"Not on your life. Besides, they wouldn't hire me anyway. I've been thinking about doing some babysitting."

Not having a resident's visa or complete command of the language and only being allowed to work a few hours a week limits my opportunities. I know he doesn't want me to do this kind of work, but we have to be realistic.

Pablo doesn't say anything for the longest time. I decide to let him ponder while I wash the lunch dishes. I've been going around and around our financial situation, and short of robbing a bank, babysitting is the only job that comes to mind.

Pablo's voice startles me. "You don't have experience dealing with children. I can find a part-time job at the university."

He follows me back to the table. We seem to live at the dinner table.

He's so busy with classes and studying, I don't see how he can find time to work. It's been hard for him to study in another language. I tell him we can't afford to have him working.

Pablo reaches for my hand. "I knew this wasn't going to be easy, but I don't want you to work in something you don't want to do."

I don't know what to say. Without words we agree there is no other choice but to babysit for the time being.

October 21

Right after Pablo leaves on Monday morning, I begin my search for the job. I'm also getting ready to model a couple of outfits at a dinner meeting next Friday. At the beginning of the semester, I joined the Graduate Structural Engineering Wives Group. I've gone to a couple of events I have enjoyed. I don't know why they chose me to model. I pray I won't be so shy and self-conscious that I'll make a fool of myself.

October 25

A babysitting job finds me through Chris. We have become good friends. She saw the ad somewhere. I'll be taking care of two children—a four-year-old boy and a three-year-old girl—while their mother works and their father goes to school. I'll begin next Monday.

An uneasy feeling overcomes me. Pablo is right. What do I know about children? I push the unwanted sensation back; a more pressing matter demands my attention. The fashion show is tonight, and butterflies flutter inside me.

The room at a restaurant, a few blocks from the university, is full of people. Where do they come from? I expect to see the group, their husbands, and maybe a few of their friends, but not all these men, women, and even children. I panic.

"Just be yourself, smile, and walk straight." I hear the voice of the woman in charge of the show. The same words she has spoken in the past few days as we prepared for the event.

Pablo is sitting at a table with a couple of neighbors who are part of the Engineering Department. He smiles at me and makes a V sign. My legs refuse to walk. Someone pushes me into the room and says, "You look great. Go show them."

I'm wearing a black dress with satin inlay in the bodice. I try to smile, but I'm sure I look like an idiot. I somehow manage to walk without falling or losing it. By the time I go out again to model a two-piece lavender outfit, I'm feeling *great!*

October 26

Did I miss my calling as a model? *Nah, my legs would have never made it,* I tell myself after last night's high. It was a nice experience, one I'm sure will not present itself again. Might as well come back to reality and get ready for church. I have a lot to do this afternoon to prepare for my new job in the morning.

CHAPTER XX

*I**ALWAYS SAW myself doing something important—whatever that meant in those idealistic years of my youth. Since writing seemed to have been in my blood forever, I thought I could begin inching my way in this most admirable field by doing something related to it. Working in a doughnut shop or doing the many other jobs I did when I came to the United States was not on my life's agenda.*

Reflecting on the jobs I held over the years, I came to the conclusion that I didn't enjoy most of them. Working for a North American publishing house in my country was probably the job I liked best. Being surrounded by books gave me the feeling of being among friends, prompting me to submerge myself into the life I craved and loved. Some of my articles and stories had already been published at this time, but my books, some in the making for a long time, waited patiently. Several are published now, my name carefully placed under different titles, giving me a sense of accomplishment.

Working as a writer was not on my mind when I first arrived in the United States. Other matters took priority, like learning a new language and earning enough money to survive. There was no room for anything else but living from moment to moment.

October 28

Will this new job end like the last one? I'll make sure it won't. We need the money. Apprehension and anxiety awoke with me this morning. *Breathe deep and don't worry,* my sensible self tells me, but my nervous self doesn't know how to relax.

I'm glad Mama and Tía María insisted I bring my overcoat and the many sweaters they pinned inside it. I still shiver as I walk the three blocks to the house where I'll be taking care of the two children. In a few weeks it'll be snowing. I heard it seldom snows in October. I can't wait though. What is it about snow that turns people into mush? I guess I'll find out when I see it.

"Good morning. I am Barbara, but everyone calls me Barb," says a tall, bony woman, ushering me inside. "I'm running late. Look in the refrigerator for whatever you need. Sandwiches will be okay for you and the children. Put them down for a nap after lunch. Children, come meet Marcela! I've got to go. I'm already late for work." She grabs her purse. "Good luck!" she yells and leaves me with a terrifying task.

I expect the children to cry and pitch a fit, but engrossed in a pillow fight, they don't pay attention to their mother or to me. I'm standing between the kitchen and the den. I don't know which one is in worse shape. The kitchen is a disaster, with dirty pots and dishes everywhere. The floor is filthy. I feel bile coming up my throat. In the den there are toys, half-full bowls of cereal, clothes, and dirt everywhere. How can people live like this?

I'm having quite a time with these children, who pretend I'm invisible and continue to do what they want. Oh, Lord! What am I doing here? This question seems to come to me when I am distressed.

"Tommy, don't you want to go to the backyard and play for a while? Come. It'll be fun."

"I don't want to." Tommy pulls Liza's hair and she begins to wail.

They hit each other until I finally separate them, put their jackets on, grab each child by the arm, and take them outside. It's nice to breathe fresh air. Soon they forget about the fight and play in a sandbox.

"It's time to come in now," I say after half an hour. "It's too cold to be outside."

Liza runs back to me, but Tommy refuses. Nothing I say seems to work. Every time I make an attempt to get hold of him, he wiggles his thin body out of my reach. He climbs up a tree and sits there, making gestures and laughing. I yell and plead to no avail. I'm concerned for his safety, but most of all, I'm mad. How can a four-year-old make fun of me like this?

I tell Tommy he can stay on top of that tree until his mother comes home, hoping to scare him, but he doesn't look at me. I figure he'll come in when he's cold enough.

I go inside with the girl and push a few dishes to make room on the counter so I can prepare sandwiches. A jar of peanut butter is the first item I see in the refrigerator. I spread it over two pieces of bread, one for each child, and pour some milk in a couple of plastic glasses. I keep on looking outside the window. Tommy hasn't moved.

While Liza eats her lunch, I see the boy coming down the tree. I hide behind the door, and as soon as he goes by, I grab him. He struggles, but I win. He barely eats his food, but I don't care.

As soon as they finish eating, I put them to bed. They are tired from it all and quickly go to sleep. I don't know where to sit for the rest of the afternoon. Eating is out of the question. I find a clean towel and put it on the sticky sofa in the den.

Barb finally comes back. This has been one of the longest days of my life.

November 4

Now I take a robe I wear over my clothes while I'm in the house of dirt. Tommy is insufferable, and with my lack of patience, I want to strangle him. I tell myself again: I have to do what I have to do when I have to do it. Thinking about it is enough to confuse me. Doing it seems to be more than I can take. Yet I'm ready to endure it since we need the money I make babysitting for food.

After several days of torture, I'm ready to tackle the impossible job of getting a visa so I can work in something else. It's going to take time to find out how to go about it, so I better make the best of this situation.

Every time I arrive at Barb's house, I feel sick. She's a nice woman who seems to want to be anywhere else but in her house, and housework must be a dirty word for her. Her husband leaves early—probably to escape the mess—so I have not met him.

Pablo stops me this morning as I'm ready to leave for my dreaded job. "I can tell you're having a hard time. You don't have to continue—"

"We don't have a choice," I interrupt him. "We need the money." I know he wants me to look for another type of job with a better environment, but I don't see how without a working visa.

"There are no options. What we need is to go to Chicago as soon as you can get away. I'm going to get a visa. I don't know how, but I will." I give him a kiss and run out the door.

There is ice on the ground. Freezing rain has been falling since early morning. I'm disappointed. I want snow. November seems to be the magic month, so it should happen soon. I walk slowly, feeling my shoes sliding over the pavement. I need to get a pair of snow boots. We have clothes warm enough for the fall but not for a cold winter. Buying winter jackets and boots is expensive. I don't know how we're going to weather the winter.

I chase the worries from my mind and concentrate on the walking, which is becoming difficult. I wait for the traffic to clear so I can cross the street. I take a couple of steps and fall. I pick myself up and try again but don't succeed.

After the fourth fall, I decide to crawl. I hope no one sees me on all fours. How ridiculous I must look. These icy roads are no fun.

"You're late and I have an important appointment. Don't do this again." Barb is frazzled and upset.

Blood rushes to my head. How dare she! "I don't think I will be late again because I won't be coming back. Since you have to go to work now, I'll take care of your children today."

Barb's face turns red and then goes pale as if going from rage to panic. "You can't do this to me. We have an understanding. I don't have time now to argue with you. We'll talk when I get back."

She leaves before I can answer. I want to tell her she never told me her house was a pigpen, her children unruly, and she is late almost every afternoon. My one-time tardiness is a big deal, but hers don't count.

Every other hour, I rehearse the speech I'm going to give Barb when she returns while I ponder on how we are going to buy groceries next week. The kids seem to sense my displeasure and behave somewhat better. I can't wait for the day to be over.

"Will you reconsider staying?" Barb asks as soon as she gets home. Her attitude surprises me. Where is the bravado?

I decide not to give her my list of complaints. "No, my decision is final. If you give me my wages, I'll be out of your way."

She doesn't move, waiting for me to change my mind. I don't move either or say anything. She finally gives up and pays me.

"Thank you, and good luck finding someone to take care of your children." I don't wait for her to try to talk me into staying. I take my leave and don't look back.

I feel light as I walk away from another job. Perhaps I'm not made for working at all. I smile. The ice has melted. I flap my wings and rush home.

CHAPTER XXI

THE FEELING OF not having the same rights other inhabitants of one country have is a strange one. The person living next door to you can work, vote, and express an opinion with unique confidence. He or she has a sense of belonging while the foreign-born feels like an intruder. This is probably one of the most devastating feelings the immigrant has to deal with.

After many years of feeling like a foreigner, I have come to terms with a situation I cannot change. As a citizen I now feel comfortable in my adopted country, giving me that elusive sense of belonging—most of the time.

Getting my resident's visa was a mystery to me. I didn't know what I was doing or asking for at the time. All I knew was that I needed that particular document in order to work. I don't know whether to cry or to laugh as I see myself as a naive but determined girl on her way to the immigration office, oblivious to what awaited her.

November 4

The thought assaults me on my way home. Is there something wrong with me? This time it wasn't the language. Am I an intolerant person? Do I object to this particular job or to jobs in general?

"I quit," I say as I walk inside the apartment, throwing my purse and robe on the sofa.

Pablo lifts his head from his books and papers and stares at me. It seems to take a long time for him to register my presence.

"What happened?" He slowly closes the book and makes a serious face.

"Even if Barb had not been unfair, I would have quit anyway. I could not have stomached that job any longer. Two weeks in that house is more than enough. I guess I'm not made for . . ." I cannot not put into words what I am trying to discern.

I know that part of it is my upbringing. No matter how hard I try, I don't seem to be able to accept jobs I consider unsuitable for me. In this country most girls over thirteen do babysitting. Why not me? It isn't that my parents are really wealthy and I can't possibly consider. It is that Latin American class thing, so difficult to explain.

Pablo walks toward me. "Don't worry. We'll manage somehow. We have so far."

I'm such a baby in spite of my good intentions. If I find a decent house and better-behaved children, I would weather the job for a time. "I'm going to fix something for dinner now. I'll tell you the whole story later."

November 6

I go about doing everyday stuff and attending my English classes two mornings a week while I look for other jobs.

It doesn't take long to find two. I hope to do better this time. Pablo keeps on telling me to forget it, but he knows we need the money, so he goes along with the idea since there seems to be no other alternative.

I go to my first job a few days after I quit the filthy house. I'm taking care of a four-year-old, a little too precocious for his age. The mother takes classes three mornings a week. The other job requires two afternoons a week, taking care of a precious little girl.

November 9

I'm still working, but last night the little girl's parents did not come home until almost eleven o'clock. She came in first, drunk. He came a few minutes later and apologized. This one is not going to work out in the long run, too bad since the little girl is a doll.

Pablo walks in that afternoon with an exciting proposal. He heard today at the university that it's possible to get a resident visa if the circumstances call for it. We're going to try to get me one so I can find a better job. Several students' wives work at the university. He hopes I can also find a job there.

"I didn't like what happened last night." Pablo's dark eyes have a weird look.

"Nothing happened to me, and I got paid for the extra time."

"I still don't like it. What if it had been the man coming drunk, alone . . . ? No. No. We're going to Chicago as soon as we can arrange it."

November 12

We are on our way to Chicago. I have the needed documentation in my bag, according to the university's office for foreign students. They gave us the information but told us we wouldn't get anywhere; a resident's visa is usually obtained in the country of origin. They are probably right. This trip may be a waste of time. But I still pray my case will fit "the special circumstance" or for a miracle.

Chicago is such a big city, we get lost several times before we reach our destination. We leave the car in a parking garage and walk with shaky legs to where we need to go.

I'm so worried I hardly make out the woman speaking to me. She asks point-blank, "Why didn't you request a visa before you left?"

"I . . . we . . . didn't know." My mind doesn't work, and I'm looking and talking like an idiot.

"I'm a student at the University of Illinois," Pablo says. "I have a Fulbright Scholarship and thought the scholarship money would be enough but . . ."

I get hold of myself, and remembering that I'm usually better than Pablo at this, I decide to let my English come to life in whatever manner and style and pray it will do the job. Besides, I am determined to do what I can to get this visa.

"The scholarship barely covers the rent and utilities. We don't have enough for food or anything else. My husband is working on his master's, and he's not going to be able to finish if I don't work . . ." I keep on talking. I have no idea what I'm telling this woman or if she understands, but whatever I'm saying brings tears to my eyes and hers.

I don't know what happened in there, but we are walking out of the building with a resident's visa, not the actual visa, which will come in the mail later, but the needed paperwork for me to begin working as soon as I find a job.

Pablo shakes his head. "Did I hear right? She did give you a visa?"

"I think so, but don't ask me. I don't know how it happened." I must have said the right words. All I know is that my prayers were answered.

"This is amazing. I never expected this to happen. You must have a wonderful guardian angel." Pablo scratches his head in disbelief.

We walk down the street without direction. It isn't registering, not yet. I'm not really aware of my being in Chicago and much less with a resident's visa under my arm.

Pablo, a big smile painted on his face, says, "We have to celebrate. I'm sure we'll find a good restaurant around here."

"One that is not very expensive." Money is becoming a thorn in my daily life.

"Let's don't worry about money today."

We walk a couple of blocks. I point to a small Italian restaurant at the corner. I know Pablo loves pasta.

Living the student's life makes me appreciate what I took for granted before. I'm enjoying the luxury of a lasagna lunch so much it's embarrassing. Pablo eats with such gusto that I can't help laughing.

He lifts his head, red sauce dripping down his chin, something Pablo hates. He grabs his napkin and wipes his face clean.

We're like two little children at a birthday party. It has been a while since we went out to eat. Our biggest outing is to take sandwiches to the courtyard and talk to the neighbors. Every so often someone invites a few of us for a drink. Pablo's studies will be our main focus for a while.

After lunch we tour the downtown area and go inside several stores. Window-shopping is all we can do for now. It's fun though. I have seen movies and heard so many stories about Chicago, gangsters, and the Mafia. I expect to see Al Capone jump from somewhere, shooting aimlessly, his suit perfectly pressed and his hat on his head. Not a hair out of place.

"It's time to head back," I say, sorry to see the day end.

We drag our feet back to the parking garage. Soon we're fighting the evening traffic. On the horizon I see Lake Michigan while my mind wanders, thinking about the immediate future. What kind of job will I find? What am I prepared to do? Going to college was always in the future, and I got married before I got started, but now working takes a priority. I type, and I know I'm intelligent, so I should be able to find something better than babysitting.

CHAPTER XXII

HAVING CHILDREN WAS in the back of my mind from the moment I got married, but the reality of it overwhelmed me each time. There is no job that requires more love, patience, knowledge, and everything a person can provide than that of being a parent. The responsibility is beyond comprehension, and yet it comes to us when we are barely out of childhood ourselves. I've always wondered about this amazing fact. I've come to the conclusion that the good Lord knows what he is doing and sends the little creatures to those who are young, have the strength to take care of them, and are willing to learn along the way.

For most people the firstborn child is almost an incomprehensible happening. No matter how much a young mother prepares herself, she has no idea what to do with the living doll in her arms. It was no different for me.

November 13

I'm still babysitting the little boy in the mornings. But today I'm going to an interview. A neighbor helped me get in touch with the computer department at the university where keypunch operators are needed.

My stomach is queasy. I'm afraid I won't understand anything. I gather my strength and I tell myself that, since I managed to get a resident's visa, I can surely get this job. I must be turning into a more mature, strong person. I walk the two blocks to where I'm going, reaching my destination with damp palms and forehead.

"Can you begin working next Monday?" the tall woman asks, looking at me with piercing green eyes.

I'm speechless. Not having said much, the question came as a surprise. I have barely given her my name and the fact that my husband is a graduate student.

"Yes." The word comes out of my mouth as if pronounced by someone else.

"Good. You'll be working three afternoons a week while you learn, then we'll see." The woman stands up and extends her hand to me. "See you next week."

I walk back home in a daze, still feeling woozy but happy to know that, finally, I have a real job. I can't wait to share my news with Pablo.

November 15

Queasiness turns into constant nausea. The smell of food spins me to the nearest bathroom almost every day. This time it doesn't seem that my cooking has anything to do with it. I've tried several remedies, but they don't seem to help.

Pablo insisted on my going to a doctor. Joanne, the neighbor married to the Arab student, provides the name of one. I made an appointment for this afternoon. My mind speculates, but I better wait. It's beginning to snow as I walk to the doctor's office, a few blocks away from the university.

"You are not sick, you are pregnant," says the doctor, a soft-spoken man with a kind smile. I like him.

"Pregnant? You mean I am going to have a baby?" I want to make sure I understand what the doctor said. My English is a lot better but a long way from perfect.

"Yes, that is exactly what I said." He smiles and looks at me in a fatherly way. "Now, let me tell you what you need to do from now on. You have to eat right, exercise, and take vitamins. I will see you once a month and . . ."

He goes on and on with an endless list of dos and don'ts. I stop paying attention. I can't think. Excitement, anticipation, worry, and a multitude of feelings and emotions crowd my being, throwing me into complete confusion.

I leave the doctor's office in a daze. Money. The fact that doctors and hospitals cost money hits me halfway home. Where are we going to get the money? Why is life so complicated? I know we're not the only young parents-to-be facing this dilemma, but it feels like it. The fact that I'll be working will help some.

I can't answer my own questions, so I keep worrying. No one ever said worrying helps, but I can't do anything else, so it will have to do.

I'm exhausted by the time I get home. I pull out the bed and decide to take a nap. I need to be rested when I tell Pablo the good news. I want to call my parents and tell the whole world about it but decide to postpone the impulse until later.

A knock brings me out of a deep sleep. I get up and drag my feet to the door.

A very pale woman with blond hair stands in front of me. "Could you come to my apartment, please? My baby is dying, and we need a godparent so he can be baptized. I believe you are Catholic."

I have a difficult time grasping what the woman means. I don't remember seeing her before. I stand there like an idiot without saying anything.

"Will you come? Please." The woman's face is tense with worry.

"Sure. Let me put on my shoes." I smooth my hair with my hand. I know I must look terrible, but the woman hurries me with her attitude.

I'm not quite awake and wonder if I'm dreaming. She rushes through the hallway and opens the door of her apartment three doors down, the same side as mine.

"Come here, please." The pale woman guides me to the back of the apartment, which is exactly like mine.

A tall, thin man and a priest stand by an infant chair containing a baby about six months old. He's paler than his mother, with a bluish tone to the skin, especially under a pair of big blue eyes. He is very thin and breathes with difficulty.

I can't take my eyes away from the baby. I feel a hole in the pit of my stomach. I'm going to be a mother like the woman holding my arm. The feeling gets to me. Dear God, take care of the baby I'm carrying. I feel tears wetting my face.

"Thank you for coming," says the tall man, who I assume is the baby's father.

The priest smiles as he takes me by the arm and walks my confused self close to the baby.

Who are these people? I look around as I try to make sense of what is happening. A baby is in danger of dying, says my brain, as I witness the sacrament of baptism. My body turns cold and my legs shake. The little boy's eyes stare at me. He has the biggest blue eyes I have ever seen. I say a silent prayer for his recovery.

The priest asks me a couple of questions I barely make out. I answer affirmative even though I don't know what he has asked. Soon the ceremony is over. There is a somber shadow in the place that weighs so heavy on my soul. I want to leave and run as far away as possible.

The mother offers me something to drink, but I can hardly swallow my own saliva. "I need to go home now. My husband is coming soon, and I need to prepare dinner. I'm sorry about the baby."

It seems to be the right thing to say. I'm sorry for the beautiful blue baby and for what the parents must be going through. I'm scared at the thoughts I don't want to let in.

"Thank you for your willingness to stand as our son's godmother," says the father as I walk to the door. Both parents walk with me.

I run to my apartment. So many feelings to deal with send me into a crying spell for some time. The shadows of the approaching night let me know it's time to think about dinner. I should make a good meal to celebrate the new life inside me. It is an occasion as special as it can possibly be.

It isn't easy to get the blue baby out of my mind and of my heart. I didn't find out the name of anyone in the family, which, in a surreal way, I have become part of. I promise myself to pay them a visit soon and ask them to excuse my silly behavior.

I get busy in the kitchen, peeling a couple of potatoes to make a potato salad I learned to do from a recipe on the mayonnaise label. I put a package of ground beef under the faucet to defrost so I can make hamburgers. Homemade hamburgers and potato salad are as good as any gourmet dinner for this important day. I believe it represents the new country where our baby will be born.

By the time Pablo walks in the door, I'm more than ready to share my news with him. I give my husband a big hug and wait for him to sit down to dinner.

He takes a big bite from his hamburger, grins, and says, "This is delicious. What's the occasion?"

"It's a big one." I wait for him to reply, but he's too busy eating. I know he didn't hear me, so I let him finish.

"Did you say a big one? What do you mean?"

"You finally registered my words in your busy mind?" I put my elbows on the table, rest my face inside my hands, and look at him. No words come to mind.

"What's going on? You are acting strangely." He turns somewhat serious.

"First I've got to tell you something interesting that happened a couple of hours ago. I became godmother of a sick baby who lives a few doors down the hall." I tell him all about the blue baby, his parents, and everything that happened that afternoon.

We talk for a while about this. Why don't I just go ahead and tell him? I want to make everything so special. He might fall asleep while I find the right moment.

"We're going to have a baby." I blurt it out, afraid of keeping it inside me forever.

Pablo opens his mouth and stares at me as if I had turned into another being, one from outer space, judging by his face. He then becomes emotional, giving the same ailment to me. Soon we're crying and embracing each other.

How we are going to pay the doctor and the hospital is not mentioned. Excitement takes over, and we dance all around the apartment. Reality and finances stay hidden in a corner somewhere, to be dealt with at a later time.

CHAPTER XXIII

GOOD PEOPLE, BAD people, interesting people, and special people have crossed my path often. Like most folks I try to stay away from those difficult human beings who insert themselves in the fabric of my life. They come and go, leaving a sour memory that often stays hidden in the wrinkles of time. There are also those special beings, who, with their love, care and understanding, stay in one's heart long beyond their presence. Several of them entered my life, our lives, at times when we most needed them.

There was a special family, like the one we met in Houston, also part of what was called host family program, who filled the void left by our faraway parents. There are no words to describe the goodness they showered on us during our stay in Illinois. They laughed with us, cried with us, accompanied us when loneliness visited, and were there for us in times of need, and there were many.

November 16

I keep telling myself that I'm going to be a mother, but it doesn't seem to sink in. I have less than seven months to prepare for this marvelous happening. The name *mother* is so big. I don't know how to react to it.

There have been so many happenings in my life lately I have almost forgotten an invitation we had a couple of weeks ago. We have postponed it twice because of classes, work and other tasks. A woman called last night to remind us about today's dinner at our new host family's home.

I am somewhat uneasy about it. This family will be in the picture longer than the one we met in Texas. What if we don't like them? We can't be so lucky that we encounter two great host families in the same year. No point in speculating. I have more important matters to occupy my mind.

"Pablo, we need to be ready in an hour."

"I'll finish this in a minute." He goes back to his books and papers.

I'm finding out that Pablo doesn't seem to have a sense of time. Before we got married, he was always late, making me very nervous, especially if we were invited somewhere. There was always an excuse, but now I see that he gets so involved in what he is doing he doesn't realize that time goes by.

I move slowly, afraid to do something that would hurt my baby. It has been only a few days since I found out about the pregnancy, but I don't feel as if I am.

I look at the map and the directions provided by the people in charge of the program. I complain about street names instead of numbers like in most cities in my country. We don't need maps to find an address there. We know that street 43 comes after 42 and *carrera* 8 after *carrera* 7.

Pablo turns his face and provides a silly smile. "Can't change the world, so might as well learn to read a map. You're my copilot."

It takes me a while, but I soon find on the map street lines with names on each one. I follow the name of the street we are on and slowly find the way to our destination in Champaign, Urbana's twin town.

"Welcome to our home," says a short woman with the prettiest smile. Her whole being seems to turn into a smile. A cheerful-looking thin man walks behind her. "We are the Williamses. My name is Kate and this is my husband, Fred. I didn't expect you to be so young."

"Pleasure to meet you," we echoed each other and follow them inside.

The house is like many others in the neighborhood, nothing special. However, from the moment we walk in, I detect a happy atmosphere, easing my misgivings.

We sit down in their den and begin talking about our families and lives as if we have known each other for years. About an hour later, two girls make their entrance.

Kate stands. "Pablo and Marcela, these are our daughters, Anne and Clare. They were at a football game."

Ann, a petite blond girl, about twelve, sits by her mother. Clare, with dark hair, sits by me. She seems to be about nine but is almost as tall as her sister. The girls look at us and smile, too shy to say more than hi.

Kate gets up and heads for the kitchen. "We'll wait a few more minutes for Steve. He's our seventeen-year-old son."

She comes back a few minutes later. "Dinner is ready. I'm warming up the rolls. We won't wait any longer."

As we sit down to eat, Steve makes his appearance. He's all feet, legs, and arms, arms that extend to all corners of the dinner table as he reaches for the food he devours faster than I can assimilate. I've never seen anyone eat so much.

"Growing boys eat enormous amounts of food." Fred looks at me and laughs. "You're not used to boys this age, I gather."

Am I that obvious? I realize my lips are half-open. "I'm sorry. I didn't mean to stare. I've a brother." My tongue tangles. I don't know what to say.

"Fred, shame on you. Leave Marcela alone."

I let the others go on talking and concentrate on eating the appetizing food on my plate: sliced potatoes, roast beef, and a vegetable casserole. Two pies sit at a nearby table. I can't wait to get a piece or two. I've noticed that my appetite has increased in the last few days. I think of food all the time even though I still have morning sickness. Steve may become a poor eater compared to me if I let myself go.

After a delightful evening we walk back to our car, followed by the whole family. "What a wonderful dinner you made for us. Thank you." I extend my hand to Fred and hug Kate.

Kate's smile gives me such comfort. I want to take her home with me. "I expect to have you over for Thanksgiving dinner."

I don't know much about Thanksgiving, but I'm sure I'll learn.

I miss my mother, father, and my whole family so much, I think as we drive back home. Frequent letters help, but it's not the same as being with them. I know I should not let myself get homesick and end up crying the whole night as I've done several times. I should be grateful for the warmth this family seems to emanate, especially now when I need my mother more than ever. How am I going to get along without my mama now that I'm pregnant? I can feel tears filling my eyes.

Pablo turns to me. "What's wrong? Didn't you have a good time? I enjoyed the evening, and the family is very nice."

"I had a great time, and I also like the family a lot. They all seem to be wonderful people. It's just that being pregnant is not only making me eat like a horse but is making me even more emotional than I already am. Don't mind me."

November 18

I talked to Papa and Mama yesterday. Mama began crying when I told her about the baby. She hopes she can come for the birth if Papa's work doesn't interfere. He won't let her come by herself. Hearing their voices shook me up badly. I haven't talked to them in a couple of months. I'm doing what I can to get hold of myself so I'll be calm to start my new job this afternoon.

The manager greets me and immediately takes me to a large room. "Nancy, this is Marcela, she's our new operator. I want you to train her. Welcome and good luck." She gives me a pat on the back and leaves.

I look at Nancy, a slender woman who stares at me. What do I know about keypunch or computers? I can't do this. I realize that every time I find myself facing a new situation, I want to run away. I breathe deeply and decide to learn the stuff if it kills me.

"This is your place." Nancy takes me to a strange-looking machine, pulls up a chair, and sits by me.

For half an hour I listen to Nancy's voice without registering what she says. It takes all my willpower to get my mind to concentrate. I'm supposed to enter data by punching it into cards fed to the machine.

"Let me know if you have any problems. Go slow at first. Someone will verify your work for errors, so don't worry." Nancy also pats me on the back. I guess she likes me, or people in this office like to make you feel good by patting you on the back.

For several minutes I stare at the machine, expecting it to reject me by doing something weird. I put my fingers on the keyboard and begin punching the information on the first card. It takes me all afternoon and several trips to Nancy's desk to get the knack of it. I'm grateful for the typing lessons I didn't like in school. I'm not a bad typist. I might be able to hold this job and not be fired or quit.

I walk home tired and yet exhilarated. A feeling of accomplishment takes me through the rest of the day. By the end of the semester I'll be finished with my English classes, so I can work longer hours and make more money. Struggling for money is not how I want to spend my life in this country or in any place. I didn't use to think much about it, but with the baby coming, it has become even more of a priority.

Pablo grabs my hand as I clear the table. "It isn't good for you to do too much. You've worked all afternoon and cooked dinner. Sit down for a moment."

"Don't you remember, I told you this morning, I have the engineers' wives' meeting tonight?"

"Are you up to it? You said the first day at work was difficult. How many holes did you punch?" Pablo is in a teasing mood.

"Let me go. I'm late. Can you take me? I don't want to walk. I'll be ready in a few minutes." I move away and rush to change clothes.

I sit with a few women I met at the last meetings. One of them modeled with me in the September gathering. At the podium someone is talking about next month's program. Tonight's speaker is a history professor. As soon as the moderator stops talking, I head for the food table and pile up a plate with finger foods. I don't understand why I'm so hungry when I just had dinner. I feel a little woozy in the mornings, but by midmorning I feel better, and then all I want to do is eat.

A thin woman I've never seen sits by me. "Hi, my name is Marion, and you are?"

I swallow a mouthful of food. "I'm Marcela."

"You have an accent. Where are you from?"

I don't like the way she says it. I guess I want to feel that I have finally conquered this tongue-twister language, but I guess it'll be a long time, if ever. I answer her question and go on eating.

"How long have you been in this country?"

"A few months."

Marion looks at me as if I were a different kind of human being. "So this is the first time you have seen buildings like we have here and attended this kind of party?"

Did she say what I just heard? It takes me a moment to think of an answer to such a stupid question. "Well, didn't you know we live on top of trees and jump from tree to tree?"

She stares at me and doesn't say anything. I'm sure she believes what I said and is trying to picture me doing the jumping. I'm so mad, but I can't help laughing. I have to learn to take stupid, ignorant comments with a grain of salt.

CHAPTER XXIV

V*IOLENCE IS A word that frightens most of us and in a twisted way seems to entertain others, at least in movie form. As a small child I was exposed to a revolution and to La Violencia, a period of years where too many lost their lives because they belonged to the wrong political party, lived in the wrong town, or were the recipients of revenge, especially in rural areas. In my country, violence has taken hold for more years than I want to count.*

For some reason the United States was supposed to be free of it, and even though bloody wars and riots had stained its soil and soul, including the assassination of a couple of presidents, I did not expect to witness one on television. I have never comprehended the use of violence in any shape or manner and never expected to see it play out in front of my eyes, not in this country.

How naive, young, and inexperienced can one be. In one way or another, violence is part of daily living throughout this land of ours.

November 22

I'm excited about Thanksgiving. I hear neighbors and people at work talking about it as if it were the most important day in the year. I believe it is good to thank God for the many graces we receive.

I've made friends at work, including Alice, a very nice woman with smiley brown eyes. She's working and also studying at the university. We take our break together and have hot chocolate with marshmallows, which I love. She is from Iowa and has been telling me all about Thanksgiving, so I can't wait to experience it with our new host family.

It's about eleven in the morning, and I don't have to work until the afternoon. I finish picking up stuff around the apartment, make up the sofa bed but don't close it, take my shoes off, and lie down. Working, going to school, and doing most everything in the apartment are making this mother-to-be very tired. I'm glad it's Friday. I plan to take lots of naps this weekend.

"What are you doing, sleeping at this time of day?" Pablo tickles my feet. Sometimes he comes in unexpectedly.

"I have to catch a nap whenever I can. Being pregnant has not only made me hungry but tired and sleepy."

"I'm going to watch television for a little while and make a sandwich for lunch. I need a break before my next class. I'm glad the Williamses gave us their old TV."

"Yes, it's good to have . . ." I hear myself mumble. I'm so sleepy I don't finish the sentence or hear anything else Pablo says. I just want to sleep and be left alone.

"MARCELA, MARCELA! WAKE UP. Something terrible is happening."

"Why are you screaming?" I jump to my feet, heart pounding.

"Somebody just shot the president."

"What?" Am I still dreaming?

"President Kennedy was shot in Dallas, Texas. He was taken to a hospital. Listen." Pablo's face is ghostly white.

"It can't be. Who? Why?" I don't get an answer because there is none. I look at my watch. It's twelve thirty.

In silence we continue watching this horrific event. Like almost everyone in this country and around the world, this charismatic president has captivated me. His wife, Jackie, visited my country recently, impressing all of us with her sophistication and classy demeanor.

I run to the kitchen for a moment to grab two pieces of bread and a piece of bologna. I don't want to miss anything, but my stomach is complaining. I'm hardly aware of what I do. I get ready to sit on the sofa bed and eat my dry sandwich when I hear the dreaded news from Walter Cronkite.

"President John F. Kennedy died a few minutes ago at Park . . . ."

I don't want to hear this. I put my hands over my ears and turn my face. How can this be true? A knot in my throat keeps me from yelling.

"This can't be happening." Pablo stands, walks to the window, and comes back.

A piece of bread is stuck in my throat. I run back to the kitchen for a drink of water. I hear Pablo saying something I can't make out. I go back to the room. We look at each other and can't think of anything to say. We just sit and listen to what Cronkite is saying. They keep on showing the shooting, Jackie Kennedy climbing on top of the car seat. It's horrible, but I can't take my eyes away from the television.

In the background I hear Pablo's voice. "I imagine there will be no classes, but I better go see. I'll be back soon."

I barely notice Pablo's leaving. I continue to be glued to the television. My brain interrupts me with a message. "It's almost time to go to work." Should I go? It seems to me almost sacrilegious to go on as if nothing happened, but with less than a week at the job, I cannot take a chance, so reluctantly, I pick myself up and get ready.

My coworkers are all punching away. Nancy looks up at me but doesn't say anything. There is an eerie silence in the big room. I look for Alice. She has her head down, but her hands are on the keyboard. I walk to her station.

"Why doesn't anyone say anything? Something terrible just happened, but no one seems to acknowledge it."

Alice's face shows sadness, but her composure amazes me. "You Latin people are so much more emotional than we are. We feel but don't show it. We go on with our lives. That's what we do."

I don't know how to stop the tears that somehow are threatening to break loose, so I don't say anything and go hide in the bathroom, where I cry softly. I regain some calm and go back to my desk.

I can't wait for the day to be over so I can go home. I can't stand so much civilized composure.

Pablo is already at the apartment, waiting for me.

"Did you have classes? You are early."

"Yes." He is silent for a moment. "Classes went on as if nothing had happened. When I asked a classmate about it, he said, 'Of course there are classes. Why wouldn't we have classes?' It is difficult to understand this kind of response."

"I had the same experience," I interrupted. "I guess different cultures react differently to extraordinary circumstances."

Every minute we have we spend it in front of the television. For some strange reason we can't seem to get enough of this incredible event. So many things take place in a few days: the funeral with a grieving wife, innocent fatherless children, and a new president. I keep on dragging the old TV set all over the apartment so I don't miss anything.

November 27

In spite of this horrible tragedy, life goes on. Tomorrow is Thanksgiving. The Williamses decided to spend this special feast with friends of theirs at a farm a couple of hours away. They invited us to go with them. We'll spend the night there and be back tomorrow after Thanksgiving dinner. I have been to many haciendas and farms, spending many Christmases and vacations at my family's hacienda, but I imagine an Illinois farm to be quite different.

We follow our host family's car out of Urbana-Champaign on our way to our first Thanksgiving, the Pilgrim's way, out in the country. Coming from a mountainous country, the flatness of this part of the land always strikes me as unreal, as if there was no end to it.

It is late afternoon when a couple with two young children greet us as we get out of the car. The man has on jeans and dusty boots. He extends his hand to me. I feel his calloused skin, the roughness left by farmwork.

"Welcome to our home. I'm Roger. This is my wife Melinda and our two children, Linda and Ronnie."

I have practiced the greeting so I would not sound like an idiot, something that happens often when I become shy and nervous in front of strangers. "Nice to meet you. Thank you for inviting us to share this holiday with you." Confident and pleased with myself, I follow everyone inside.

I go for a comfortable-looking chair while everyone else finds a seat somewhere in a rustic, cozy room. Glasses of lemonade circulate. Pablo sits on the sofa near me. We look at each other in expectation.

"Please, make yourselves at home while I take care of tonight's dinner." Melinda's sturdy tall figure moves toward the kitchen. "We go to church on Thanksgiving Eve. I trust you want to accompany us."

It seems more like an order to me. She didn't say what kind of church. I'm sure it'll be another experience for me. For some strange reason Melinda fascinates me with her I-can-do-everything look. She appears strong, healthy, ready to tackle the work of five people or more. It must be the good air and healthy living.

"Can I help you?" asks Kate, getting up.

I follow suit. "I'll be happy to help you too."

"Sit down, please. You're our guests. Linda, come."

The little girl jumps to her feet and follows her mother.

Ten minutes later we all sit around the dining table. It's so good to eat fresh food, just like we did at home. I'm sure they had killed the chicken that morning and picked the vegetables from the ground in the backfield. Everything tastes great. It surprises me that there were few comments on the assassination.

"It's time to go to church. Are you coming with us?" The question comes from Roger, who waits for our answer.

"Yes, of course." My response can't possibly be anything else. Pablo and I had already agreed in that silent talk married couples seem to develop and perfect along the way.

I know I will feel strange like I did in Houston. I put on my jacket and wait for directions.

Roger opens the back door for us. "You can ride in our car. I don't want you to get lost. The Williams family will follow."

This church is not like the one in Houston. It looks like a very nice courtroom where you expect a judge to preside. There is nothing that would identify it as a church, no cross or anything. It's quite an elegant place for a small town, with beautiful wood panels. There is a long sermon, and people sing a couple of hymns. This time I don't feel strange. I just feel like I am in a meeting, not inside a church. I still have a lot to learn about religion in this country.

It's very dark by the time we go to bed. It reminds me of nights at the hacienda. When my siblings and I were children, we used to scare each other in the dark. I'm tired and go to sleep as soon as I hit the pillow. I don't think I move until I wake to a cold gray day. I find it proper for the occasion.

November 28

I feel sorry for Melinda and her young daughter. They have been working all morning, fixing breakfast and preparing the big meal. The little girl is too young to be doing so much work. She peels potatoes, washes vegetables and dishes, and yet seems content. The little boy helps his father with firewood for the fireplace. The Williamses' children are probably outside or sleeping.

The idea of having food around all day appeals to me. My morning sickness is almost gone, and my appetite increases all the time.

It's fun to get to know the Williamses better and to experience life in the country.

After a delicious breakfast, Roger takes Pablo and me to see the milking cows, the pastures, and vegetable garden.

"You don't have people working here?" I ask at not seeing anybody around, probably because it's a holiday.

"Sometimes a couple of men from town come to help when we have to plow or do some big job." Roger arranges things in the stable.

"In the big haciendas in my country there are many people working the land. We call them *peones*."

Roger smiles as if I had said something funny. "We could not afford them. Labor is expensive here. All of us work the farm, even the children. We are up early in the morning to begin the milking." He pauses and looks at me for a moment. "You look cold and tired. Pregnant young ladies need to rest. Why don't you go to the house and have a warm drink."

I know Roger thinks I'm a wimp. I'm sure Melinda worked through her pregnancies. I go back to the house while Pablo and

Roger continue touring the property. Life seems so difficult for these people. I suddenly realize how tough it is for farmers, peasants, and workers around the world, especially the poor in undeveloped countries.

I've never seen so much food on a table. A sumptuous turkey, potatoes of different colors— they tell me the orange ones are sweet potatoes—corn, and so many other delicious-looking edibles make my eyes grow big and my stomach happy with anticipation. I hope I don't get sick. One of my favorite dishes turns out to be the cranberry sauce, a new type of food for me.

After an incredible Thanksgiving dinner, almost everyone sits in front of the television to watch football games. I don't understand the first thing about it, so I go help Melinda and her daughter with the dishes.

Full and happy to have experienced such an important feast for the people of this country, we drive back home, taking with us the essence of the Pilgrim story.

CHAPTER XXV

THE IMAGES OF Christmases gone by fill me with nostalgia, happiness, and a feeling of gratitude for having experienced them. My extended family usually got together in the big hacienda where we built a pesebre, *the biggest nativity we could manage. The lighting of fireworks thrilled all of us. The midnight dinner with turkey one year and big tamales the next made us quite international. Of course, as a child, the most exciting of all was waiting for baby Jesus, who deposited toys on the bed while we slept.*

As an adult, this meaningful holiday changed. There were still years when the extended family got together at the hacienda. Other times circumstances forced us to spend the holidays either in the city or, in our case, in another country, having to adapt to other customs and celebrations. We have managed to merge the two cultures, keeping the pesebre *and foods from the past, along with the Christmas tree, carols, and the illusion of snow, when not available.*

We couldn't see ourselves spending that first Christmas in the United States alone, so we figured a way to visit friends in Boston, not ready to completely change our ways yet.

December 8

I need to stop eating like a horse, but I don't know how. The holiday season—which here seems to go from Thanksgiving to after New Year—is not helping any. Different groups at the university have been inviting us to parties and gatherings, making my stomach very happy but not the little voice inside me telling me to stop the gluttony. My small waist that I have always been so proud of is no longer small.

"We should go somewhere for Christmas," Pablo says while we eat breakfast.

It's Sunday, and I want to go back to bed. "You're always coming up with trips and things we can't afford. Besides, where can we go?"

Pablo finishes eating his cereal before he answers. "Don't you remember that Max and his family are in Boston, where he's working on his master's?"

"Yeah, I forgot about them. They left before we did. Still, it's expensive to travel to Boston."

Max is one of Pablo's best friends. They went to college together. It would be nice to see them though. They got married before we did and have two little girls. There is a bit of excitement somewhere inside me.

Pablo tells me he has seen ads at the university asking for rides to different parts of the country for the holidays. He plans to look for a student who wants to go ride with us and share expenses.

Kate Williams invited us to spend Christmas with them, but Pablo thinks we can't impose ourselves on them all the time. Even though they seem to enjoy our company, he doesn't want us to become unwanted pests.

Pablo is getting more excited by the minute. He finds a calendar somewhere. We spend the rest of the afternoon planning and anticipating a most wonderful trip.

December 9

Pablo walks in on Monday evening with his mouth full of news he burps out as soon as he steps inside the apartment. He found a student who wants to go to Maine. He'll go with us to Boston and then take a bus to his hometown. We'll leave the end of next week. He rushes to call Max.

December 21

We're on our way early Saturday morning, along with Douglas, an overweight man with an unfriendly face. I hope the car behaves.

After all, it isn't new. I'm grateful Pablo is good at fixing cars if we need it. He bought a few tools, just in case.

"It's cold today. I hope the roads are free of ice. It's so treacherous to drive on slippery roads." Pablo's voice is soft, directed to me.

"You mean you don't know how to drive on icy roads?" Douglas yelled from the back.

"I'm a careful driver, so don't worry."

We don't talk for the longest time. Douglas doesn't seem to want to exchange words with us. I've tried a couple of times to make conversation that he barely acknowledges, answering with monosyllables, so muteness takes over as Pablo concentrates on driving and I look at the flatlands.

My stomach begins to growl. "I'm hungry. Can we stop to eat something?"

Douglas digs inside a grocery bag he has with him. "I brought the food I need for the trip. We don't need to stop."

"You may not need to stop but we do. My wife is pregnant and needs to move around a little. We also need to eat."

Waving a sandwich, Douglas says, "We didn't agree to stop every few hours. You should have brought some food to eat on the road."

Pablo pulls over at a Howard Johnson restaurant. "We agreed to share expenses, not to drive straight through. You can come if you want or wait for us. Your choice."

We walk out without looking back. I'm glad our bags are in the trunk and Pablo has the keys. I don't trust this man. I've budgeted a few dollars for frugal meals. I should have thought to bring some prepared food, at least for the first meal. It would have saved us some money. I'm still not practical enough to think of these things.

On our way out we see Douglas sitting on a bench by the door, waiting for us. He has a murderous look. He doesn't say a word and runs to the car. I bet he was freezing and had to go inside the restaurant.

We drive for hours without saying much. Our passenger makes us so uncomfortable we don't feel free to talk or do anything.

"You're driving too slow," Douglas says as daylight flirts with late afternoon shadows. "We'll never make it to the next city at this speed."

"Did we also agree to drive at a certain speed?" Pablo's face turns red. "If we have to stay at a motel, we'll do that. I'm not going to get in an accident for you."

"I'm not paying any motel room. We're going straight to Boston as agreed."

Pablo doesn't comment, which gives me some relief. Last thing we need now is a big fight in the middle of a freeway.

We drive through the night. I'm exhausted. Every time we stop for a cup of coffee and much-needed rest, Douglas turns into a monster ready to devour us. We decide not to pay attention to him.

December 22

By the end of the second day, we arrive in Boston. I can't think. Why is it that every time we take a trip in this country, we end up traveling for days, arriving at our destination half-dead and looking like old rags?

"This is the end of the agreement." Pablo stops the car in front of the Greyhound station and turns to Douglas. "You can find whatever mode of transportation you can. We're not driving back with you. I won't risk my wife losing our baby because of you. Good-bye."

"You can't do that. We have an understanding. If I had the money for a bus, I would have taken it."

"With your attitude, you should not be traveling with human beings." I can't help giving him a piece of my mind.

"I'll be waiting here on the appointed day." Douglas is out of the car, standing on the sidewalk with his luggage.

"Don't do it. We won't be here. Have a happy holiday season if you can." Pablo puts the car in gear and drives away.

"What a nightmare." My voice comes out so soft I can't hear myself talk. I can't believe we have lived through this ordeal. Life brings such unexpected happenings.

"Are you okay?" The concern in Pablo's eyes gives me a little push to survive until we find our friend's address.

"I guess I'm well enough, considering how terribly tired I am."

December 23

A good night's sleep and being with friends from the country we left several months ago, which now seems more like years, make me feel great, even though I didn't sleep enough to recover. I soon forget about being tired and prepare myself for a few days of sharing good times.

We talk all day, make sandwiches for lunch, and take care of the little ones. Late in the evening we decide to go to dinner to a family restaurant where we can take the children.

"Marcela, be careful of the ice. Don't walk so fast."

Pablo isn't finished with the last word when I slip, landing on my rear. "Why did you say that? Your words tripped me." Max and Pablo help me up, and we continue walking; this time Pablo is holding me.

The fall frightens me. My body has taken a lot of abuse in the last couple of days. I pray that my baby is okay and promise to be more careful.

It is snowing hard by the time we get out of the restaurant, where we had our fill of good Boston food. Big flakes land on us as we walk to the car. Like a little kid, I grab a handful of snow and make snowballs. Soon we are all throwing them at each other, enjoying nature's generosity with the white stuff we so much enjoy, forgetting my promise to be careful.

December 24

It's Christmas Eve, the night we celebrate Jesus's birth. Max and Luz have a small *pesebre* in their fireplace, giving us the feeling of a Christmas at home. It isn't the same as being at the ranch with our families, but it's wonderful to be able to share this important holiday with good friends. It's our first Christmas with snow, just like in the movies. We go out for a while to listen to a group of people sing Christmas carols. Luz puts the children to bed early. We stay up eating, drinking wine, and enjoying the newness of a different experience. A melancholy feeling grips me every so often, but I won't let it linger. I'm adamant about enjoying our first Christmas in this country. During the next few days, we tour the city so rich in history.

December 31

Our visit comes to an end too soon. I had such a wonderful time. I'm not ready to leave this marvelous city. I embrace Luz, who holds me tight. She is as homesick as I am. We talked at length one evening on how difficult it is to leave your homeland and adjust to another culture.

"I hope you come visit us before you go back home." I address both of them.

Max is helping Pablo with the luggage. "It'll be difficult to come your way with a baby and a toddler, but you never know. I'm very glad you were able to come. You made our Christmas so special."

Tearing myself away from friends and the comfort of a situation reminiscent of my old familiar life isn't easy. We drive in a quiet mood for a while. My thoughts go south in the map of the Americas, stopping at the country of my birth, visiting those familiar places that made my daily living not long ago.

Pablo suddenly breaks the silence. "Do you think Douglas is really waiting for us at the bus station?"

"He said he would. I hope he doesn't get too upset and makes us pay somehow."

"I imagine he's not very happy, but it's his own doing. We had the best intentions . . ." Pablo's face shows signs of worry for a moment. "Let's forget about Douglas and enjoy the trip."

We had talked about spending New Year's Eve at a hotel. We would have stayed in Boston, but we both have to be back right after New Year's Day.

"We're going to have to find an inexpensive hotel." It seems to be my job to handle the money and worry about it. We barely have enough to make it back home. Since Douglas is not paying expenses for the return trip, we're really short of funds.

Pablo and money don't seem to mingle well, so he keeps quiet.

We take it easy and stop whenever we feel like it. It's heavenly not to hear Douglas telling us not to stop or eat or drive too slowly.

For the last couple of hours, I've been struggling with a nagging headache, so I ask Pablo to stop in the next city.

It's almost ten at night when we find a small and cozy hotel in Cincinnati, which will eat up most of our money, but what the heck, we have to welcome the New Year in style.

"Do you feel like going down to eat?" asks Pablo.

"No, I'd rather rest here for a while. You go ahead if you want. Bring me a sandwich or whatever you find."

Pablo touches my forehead. "I hope you're not coming down with something. I'll bring dinner here."

I close my eyes and lean against the pillow on the bed but can't find a comfortable position. Not able to find a cure for my aching head, I sit and wait for Pablo.

He really splurges and brings a couple of thin steak dinners we truly enjoy. After we eat, I take a painkiller and almost immediately go into a deep sleep.

"Marcela, get up. It's midnight. Is your headache gone?"

"I think it's almost gone." The moon shines outside the window, embracing us in its silver rays.

"HAPPY NEW YEAR!" we say at once.

We embrace and kiss and wish for everything wonderful to happen to us, especially for a healthy baby. It's such an unlikely celebration that I figure I'm dreaming it.

January 1

Later than expected we hit the road the next day. It's a beautiful morning. The snow shines under the sunrays. The little girl inside me is delighted with the sight. We go on driving for hours.

It's almost three in the afternoon, and we have not eaten since breakfast. Pablo slows down as he looks for a place to grab a bite.

"We have a problem. I've been watching the gasoline gauge and it's coming down fast. We may have to choose between eating and putting enough gasoline in the car to get back home. We only have a couple of dollars left."

Pablo looks at the gauge, thinks for a few moments, and says, "We have enough gas. We're not very far. Let's eat."

We stop at a fish-and-chips place. We pay one dollar and fifty cents for a couple of pieces of fried fish we gobble with gusto.

We're back on the road, my eyes fixed on the gas gauge, while I pray we won't be left stranded in the middle of the road. To ease my worries I begin to sing. Pablo goes along with the singing.

Still singing, with less than fifty cents in our pockets and an empty gasoline tank, we arrive home followed by the shadows of the night.

CHAPTER XXVI

HAVING VISITORS FROM abroad, especially from my country, has always been a source of great joy. Over the years, family and friends have come in and out of our home in whatever city we happened to live, and we have lived in many, including several years spent back in our country. During those years, we enjoyed the luxury of being with parents and siblings before heading back to the United States for good.

With the passing of time, members of both families died, and others moved away from the close nest we knew. In my grandparents' era, families in Latin America lived in the same city, usually a few doors down the road or close-by, if not in the same family home. During my parents' time, family members began to move to other cities within the country, visiting the ancestral home as often as possible and spending long days together. Then we began moving to other countries, and now we are scattered throughout the world as many families are. Even visiting is not an occurrence that happens often.

I crave those lazy vacation days when the whole family, old and young, got together at the hacienda or at my grandmother's home, told stories, played games, and sipped lemonade as if the canvas of that moment in life would always be the same.

January 9

I enjoy being home, but loneliness has come to visit. Our courtyard gatherings stopped when it turned cold, and the neighbors seem to be hibernating. Hot chocolate with Alice is the highlight of my day. I miss going to visit family and friends and the many social gatherings back home.

I like cold weather, but this is a little too cold for me. I don't have the right clothes and have to pile sweatshirts and sweaters on my cold body to keep warm. My overcoat is of no use now. Pablo found a bargain jacket for himself. We're going this afternoon to get one for me. I also need boots so I don't keep slipping when I walk on ice.

Mama, aunts, and everyone we know are sending the cutest clothes for the baby. Little embroidered shirts, so delicate I'm afraid to touch them, handmade blankets and sheets, sweaters, bibs, and other baby items. It's so much fun going down to the mailbox to find a package, and sometimes two, that I'm disappointed when I don't find any. How I wish they could all share this time with us. If I dwell on not having my family with me when the baby is born, I will become so sad I can't stand it.

"Where did you get all these magazines?" Pablo picks up the bundle I found in the mailbox this afternoon.

"I have no idea where they came from. They all have our name but we have not ordered them."

Pablo looks at the issues of *Parents, Redbook, Reader's Digest,* and others, six of them. "Are you sure you didn't order them?"

"Of course I am. Why would I order something we don't want? This is most puzzling."

Pablo throws the magazines on the table. "Why do I have the feeling that this is the way our crazy passenger is taking revenge on us? I bet you Douglas is doing this."

"Have you seen him?"

"No, I haven't. He studies languages in another part of the campus. I never saw him before I contacted him for the trip. I hope I don't see him again to avoid what's coming to him."

January 20

All kinds of magazines continue to appear in the mailbox. I'm so angry. I find myself yelling inside the apartment. I've been returning them for weeks. I don't ever want to see another issue of a magazine. We can't be sure Douglas is the guilty party, but I'm ready to agree with Pablo, even though we may never find out.

"Guess who's coming to visit us?" I hand Pablo the letter I've been holding since I heard him coming down the hall. I've been listening for his steps for a while. I let him read about Tía María's visit. "She's coming early in February."

His face glows as he reads the letter. Pablo has always been Tía María's favorite nephew. She writes to us almost every week. I like her a lot. She's been very nice to me, unlike his mother, who would have rather kept him by her side forever and has been somewhat distant, to put it mildly.

This apartment is too small. I look around it. Where are we going to put her? All kinds of possibilities have crossed my mind, like putting a partition between the sofa bed and the dining area, but there is no room for a bed.

We discuss applying for a one-bedroom apartment. It comes with a sofa bed in the living room, like the one we have here, and has a furnished bedroom. When the baby comes, we'll have to move anyway. We'll just do it a little early.

How much more will it cost? I worry. Being in charge of finances is turning me into my mother who also manages the money. My father, like Pablo, doesn't like to deal with it.

Pablo is going tomorrow to the Housing Department to find out if there is an apartment available.

January 24

It takes a couple of days before we get a response from Housing. The wait pays off. We can move the first of the month, just a few days before Tía María arrives. We'll move one floor down, toward the end of the hallway. It'll be nice to have a separate bedroom and an actual living room. The best news is that the rent is less than I expected.

I let some of my neighbors know we're moving. The little boy down the hall is still alive. He looks pretty much the same, thin and bluish. I've been so afraid to learn otherwise; I have not been to see him since his baptism.

February 1

Moving day is here. My friend Chris and her husband are helping us move. I'm glad we don't have any furniture to haul from floor to floor. We bump into each other as we try to walk among boxes and suitcases.

Pablo rushes through the apartment in search of a pair of scissors to tape the boxes. This morning he borrowed a dolly from the library but can only keep it for a few hours, so he's all over the place, making me nervous.

"Aren't you glad I have everything packed and ready?" I don't get a response. Pablo is too busy looking for the scissors. I get them for him.

"Hi, are we late?" Our friends walk in wearing sneakers, jeans, and a neighborly attitude.

This couple has been our guardian angels since the day Chris knocked at my door with a welcoming plate of food. Most of our neighbors have been nicer than I ever dreamed of.

In less than three hours we have moved everything. Pablo and Ken leave to return the dolly. Chris goes to her apartment to get supper ready. I can't believe she's doing so much for us.

I wish I could cook like Chris. For tonight's dinner she brings meatloaf, potato salad, and peas. She even baked a coffee cake. I enjoy every bite. We clear the table and call it a day.

I'm beginning to show, feeling heavier than I look and more tired than I can afford to be. I gather enough energy to make the bed and throw myself in it. I know I'll be asleep as soon as I close my eyes.

February 4

Tía María emerges from the plane, wearing her hat and gloves and carrying her purse. She belongs to the generation of women who can't go out of the house without her hat and handbag. She hugs Pablo for the longest time.

It's so wonderful to see family. I get all shook up. We embrace. "Did you have a good trip?"

"Long but good." She goes back to Pablo and holds his hand. "It takes a lot of traveling and changing planes to come to Chicago."

Pablo holds her arm. "This way, Tía. We need to get your luggage. I'm glad you didn't have all the problems we had. It was a nightmare."

"I know, Marcela told me all about it. My poor babies, no wonder we were so worried when you left. Marcela, let me see you." She inspects me from head to toe. "You look like a mother should."

I don't know how to take her assessment. Knowing her, I'm sure she meant it as a compliment. Tía María, a bacteriologist, is the oldest of six siblings, many years older than Pablo's mother. She loves to travel.

She puts her hand on my shoulder for a moment and tells me I look pretty and happy. This is music to my ears.

Pablo tries to speed up her pace, but it takes us forever to go down to baggage. She walks with short steps, slower than I remember.

Tía María looks tired and dozes off all the way home. It is late evening by the time we get back. Last night I prepared a casserole with ground beef, corn, breadcrumbs, and other ingredients from a recipe Chris gave me. She made a pie for the occasion.

"This is one of the best meals I've had. I didn't know you cooked this well."

Pablo laughs. "She has come a long way from the blood-running chicken, strange pizza, and other cooking catastrophes."

"You were not any better, so don't make fun of me."

I'm still waiting for him to learn to cook anything. He says he's an expert at opening cans of soup and dumping an egg inside, cooking it to perfection.

February 5

The next day we take Tía María around the campus. With her tiny steps, she walks from one end to the other while she shivers, but she doesn't complain. She never does. I have asked for a couple of days off from work so I can spend time with her since Pablo can't skip classes.

With her hat on her head and her handbag and gloves, she is ready to go to the Williamses' house for dinner, a couple of days after her arrival. I'm grateful for the invitation since we have run out of places to show her.

On our way back, after a delightful evening, Tía María talks about how much she likes the Williamses. She says she feels peace of mind, knowing we have good people looking after us since our families can't. There is sadness in her voice. I know she misses us as much as we miss her. My heart aches for those I love.

February 17

The day for Tía María to leave sneaks up on us. We had two wonderful weeks with her. We are now on our way back to the airport.

"I wish you weren't leaving." I hug her tight. It has been so wonderful to have her with us; I hate to see her go.

"I . . . It was . . ." Pablo's words get lost in the emotion of the moment, his face buried in a long hug.

Tears fill Tía María's eyes as she disappears on her way to the airplane.

We sit in front of the window and wait until the plane takes off. In deep thought and silence, we walk out of the airport and drive back to Urbana.

CHAPTER XXVII

ENTERTAINING IS SOMETHING I enjoy once the house looks perfect, the table is set as I envisioned it, and the food turns out great. Before all of this I'm a nervous wreck. At times I'm so tired I just want to go to bed. I envy those who take entertaining with a grain of salt, without worrying.

After many years of struggling to serve the perfect dinner or have the flawless party, I have come to terms with my inadequacies to accomplish this kind of feat by myself. I can do a decent job with trained maids and the help of elders in the family or anyone willing to give me a hand.

Still, I strive for the best I can possibly manage, which I have done for years. I envision a maid with a white apron over a black dress to serve our guests. My first dinner party as students was a party to remember.

March 26

As much as I enjoy the snow, I'm glad winter is almost over. By the middle of March, I was ready to see green around me and get rid of so much dirty black ice and snow along sidewalks.

I find winter and summer in this country either too cold or too hot. I'm not used to extreme temperatures. The place where I was born is one of the few in the world where springlike temperature reigns throughout the year.

March is almost gone without much ado. Magazines subscriptions finally stopped appearing in our mailbox after I contacted almost every magazine in the country. Clothes for the baby still come, not every day but at least once a week. We'll only need to buy diapers and a bassinet. I've become an expert at keypunching while my figure has turned into a balloon.

"Pablo, the parents of my godson invited us for Easter dinner," I tell him as he comes in for lunch. We try to have lunch together when he doesn't have classes.

This invitation surprised me. I have not been a good godmother. I think I'm afraid to get too close to these people. It'll be too painful when . . .

"I thought we were going to go to the Williamses'." He opens a can of soup while I fix sandwiches. "I don't know those people. It's going to be awkward for me." This is his typical reaction when faced with a new social situation.

I let him know I already called Kate and told her about this other invitation. "I feel we should accept. After all, I'm the baby's godmother. They are good people. Anyway, sometimes we have to do what doesn't sound exciting because it's the right thing to do. I know we'll enjoy it. I'll get a present for the baby. I owe him one."

"Okay. If we have to."

March 29

The days before Easter Sunday are busy with work and Holy Week services, which we try to attend as we have done since we were children. It's very different here, though. Everybody works and goes on with their daily affairs as if it is a week like any other. It isn't for me. This is God's week.

Easter Sunday is a bright, cold day. I want to wear something nice, but I now look like a huge pumpkin. I choose a white and green maternity top, the best I can find among my small maternity wardrobe. I do what I can to hide my bulging stomach, get ready for Easter Mass and then go to the neighbors' apartment.

"We're so glad you could come. We're Bill and Liza," says Bill as he opens the door. "We don't know each other's names even though you are our son's godmother."

We go over our names and introductions, and I apologize for everything I didn't do.

The little boy is bigger but looks the same, thin and blue. He smiles at me. I hold his hand, wanting to make him understand how much I want him to be healthy. I play with him for a few moments, but he only smiles without moving much. I can see his chest going up and down. Pablo stares at him and then sits.

I give Liza a baby toy and after a short chat, we move to the dining table.

Pablo seems to be enjoying himself talking to Bill about planes while I enjoy the delicious dinner. Bill is an army pilot.

Liza passes the ham to Pablo. "We're happy to have you share this day with us. We're all away from home, and getting together helps during the holidays. When is your baby due?" I see the sadness in her eyes. I so feel for her.

"In June. I know I look as if I'm having it tomorrow, because I've been eating like a pig, gaining all the weight in the world."

They laugh and say I look terrific and all those things people say to make you feel better. I am glad for the lighthearted moment. Liza puts the baby to sleep. We visit a while longer before we leave this nice and sad family.

April 4

A week later Pablo announces he has invited one of his professors and his wife to dinner next Saturday.

"You invited people here? Why didn't you ask me? I don't think I can cook for company. What am I going to do? I wish Mama were here."

I'm annoyed with Pablo for not checking with me, and yet I knew the day would come when we would have real guests. In Austin, our friends from Chile were neighbors, and when we visited, we just threw meals together. I miss our little gatherings. We had so much fun. We received a Christmas card but have not heard from them since, the same with Inéz and the colonel.

"You worry too much. We're students, so I'm sure the professor doesn't expect a fancy dinner. Let's just make spaghetti. Nothing to it."

I don't answer. Men. I run to the kitchen to look for my cookbooks. Two were given to me at one of the bridal showers and another I bought at a sale, hoping it would give me the push I need.

Everything looks difficult and expensive. I put the books aside and begin preparing tonight's supper, a simple dinner of rice, pork and beans, and tomatoes. Not very appetizing, but I can't think of anything else.

April 10

Saturday's dinner has been on my mind for days, and I still don't know what to prepare. I may have to go for the spaghetti. I remember seeing a recipe for Spaghetti a la Diabla. Tomorrow is Saturday, so I don't have any more time to think of something better.

After work I go to the store and buy pasta, sauce ingredients, chicken, red pepper—supposedly the most important ingredient—lettuce, tomatoes, etc. I go home and put everything on the counter for tomorrow. I'll have all day before company arrives.

April 11

I can't sleep. My stomach is in the way. Sometimes the baby kicks hard and wakes me up. It's morning, but I'm tired and don't feel like getting up. I doze off, but my nervousness doesn't let me sleep, dragging me out of bed to begin the day.

Pablo has gotten up early and seems ready to leave. I knew he would go to the library, leaving me to deal with everything that has to be done. I'm having a difficult time accepting the roles of maid and cook. I'd much rather go to college. "Your turn will come, now go to take care of the day," says a little voice inside me.

"I've to go to the university library for a while to do research on a paper due in a week. I'll be back soon. Do you need anything?"

"Yes, a cook will do. I'm a nervous wreck. I don't move as easily as before I was pregnant. It's going to take me all day to get everything ready. I can use your help. What time is company coming?"

"About six thirty. Relax and don't worry. I'll try to come back as early as possible."

The hours disappear faster than I can count. I've cooked the chicken, the sauce, and the spaghetti. I'm rushing to make the salad when I hear Pablo come in.

"I'm sorry I'm so late, but this paper is really tough. How are you coming along?"

"Don't ask and help me set the table."

The telephone rings. Pablo goes to answer it. "It's Chris, for you."

I ask him to mix the pasta with the sauce and the chicken while I take the call. I talk to Chris for a few minutes and rush back to the kitchen.

"I guess you left the red pepper by the stove for me to also mix with the pasta."

"You added more red pepper? OH! NO. NO! I didn't ask you to do that. I already put enough."

"Well, it was there . . ." Pablo, the pot of spaghetti in his hand, freezes for a moment. "Let me try it."

He spoons out a handful of pasta and shoves it in his mouth. I wait in expectation. His face turns red and he has a coughing fit. He drinks a glassful of water and tries to talk, but only a guttural noise comes out of his mouth.

It's not edible. What are we going to do? Before I can say anything the doorbell rings.

"They're here. It's only six." A panic sound comes out of Pablo's hoarse voice.

"You probably told them to come at six. Go, open the door and entertain them while I think of something."

I rush and put the rolls in the oven, pour dressing on the salad, and put it in the refrigerator while I wait for the Holy Spirit to give me a tip of what to do with this very spicy meal. *Make another sauce and wash the pasta and the chicken*, my mind responds. I let water run over the pasta.

Pablo sneaks up behind me. "Come say hello. They are asking for you."

I wash my hands and smooth my hair. I had planned to change clothes and fix myself, but at this point, it doesn't matter how I look; it will have to do. Being pregnant is a good excuse.

I'm in such panic; I can hardly focus on the professor and his wife. He is thin and wears glasses, and his wife has on a red-and-white dress and also wears glasses. All I can think about is the washed-out spaghetti waiting for me in the kitchen. If they only knew.

I stay a few minutes and then get up, excuse myself, and run back to the kitchen.

For a moment I stand there, looking at the now-white pasta. Praying for another can of sauce, I open the cabinet. I find one hidden in the back of several cans of soup. My feet are swollen and painful.

I prepare the sauce, drain the now soggy spaghetti and chicken, and mix it. I taste it. It's still spicy but not terribly.

"Did you fix it?" Pablo has already come twice to rush me.

"Dessert. I didn't think about it."

"Why did I think I could invite people over?" He throws his arms up in desperation. "This is turning into a fiasco. I'll go to the store and get some ice cream. Come out for a moment and visit with them until I get back." He turns around and leaves.

A burning smell stops me on my way out of the kitchen. "The rolls," I yell.

"Can I help?" asks a woman voice from the front room.

"No, thank you. I'll be right there." The rolls are dark brown. I take them out and go to see about our mystified guests. I go in and out of the kitchen three times to check on a dinner that should not be served to a dog before Pablo comes back with the ice cream. These people must think we are nuts or stupid.

While I finish setting the table—Pablo didn't have time to do it—I see the woman glancing at me as if she were trying to understand this foreign couple who can't put a simple meal together.

It's time to serve them what I can. I pick out the rolls that don't look too bad, pour the pasta in a silver platter I brought from home—how ironic—and take the salad out of the fridge. The lettuce is wilted. I should not have bathed it with the dressing, I guess. I take a fork and try to revive it, putting tomato wedges on top.

"Dinner is ready," I announce.

We sit down to eat washed, soggy spaghetti, burnt rolls, and wilted salad. The only food I didn't ruin is the ice cream. We hardly talk during dinner. I see Pablo, his professor and wife struggling to swallow this horrible food. I want to hide under the table.

Presto, after we finished eating, alleging another engagement, the abused couple leaves.

I throw myself on the sofa. "This is one of the worst days I've ever had."

"Yeah, short of a hanging. I can't believe everything went wrong."

When something like this happens, people say you'll laugh at it later. Right now I don't feel like laughing. I don't think I'll ever forget this evening.

Exhausted from work and tension, we clean up and pile everything in the sink. I can't endure the kitchen any longer.

Before turning off the light I say, "I will never have company again until we get back home and have maids." Not waiting for a comment, I turn off the lamp, close my eyes, and refuse to think any more about my dinner fiasco. As a hostess I still have everything to learn.

CHAPTER XXVIII

THERE ARE TIMES in my life when I feel out of touch with reality. It usually happens when something extraordinary is about to occur. Life turns into a whirl of out-of-control emotions, and I have the feeling of not being able to get hold of whatever has taken over my being.

This eerie sensation has visited me every so often. At times I don't know what causes it, but in others instances, it is brought on by a death and illness in my family, a change in life so great that the floor under my feet seems to move. It's almost like a dream where I have no control. The move to the United States and the last month of my first pregnancy made me feel this way.

May 21

I drag my body from place to place. I can't wait to get back to my normal light self. I've gained almost thirty pounds, putting a heavy strain on my small frame. It's difficult to sit for long periods, making work hours strenuous. I want the baby to come, and yet I'm terrified. I can't imagine how childbirth will be.

I'll work until Friday of next week. For a couple of months, I'll stay home with my child. We receive unexpected and helpful gifts from the family.

May is coming to an end. The trees are green, and flowers are appearing everywhere. I walked to the doctor this morning for my monthly checkup, enjoying the beauty of spring that gave me a wonderful lift.

"The doctor says the baby is coming soon." I tell Pablo at dinnertime. As I say this, my heart jumps with joy and fear.

Pablo stops eating and looks at me strangely as if the reality of the baby suddenly hits him for the first time. He mumbles something and goes back to his food. I know how he feels.

To change the subject, I inform him about Kate's invitation to a picnic next Saturday. It's still a little cool for a picnic, but nature's lushness is hard to resist. It'll be nice to spend a few hours in a park.

After clearing the table and washing dishes, I take out the smallest bag we own and pack what the hospital suggested. I pack and unpack a couple of times then put the bag aside, too tired to think of what else I may need. I decide to call it a day and go to bed.

May 22

It's another clear and cool morning. I walk to the store to get a few groceries. Even though I have more than three weeks, according to the doctor, I want to make sure there is food in the house while I am at the hospital. I get the mail on my way back to the apartment. There is a letter from Mama. I receive one from her almost every week. I rush upstairs to read it—if moving a little faster can be called rushing.

> My dear Marcela:
>
> I so want to be with you when your baby comes. It'll be our first grandchild, and I would have given anything to share this time with you, but you know your father. He thinks I'll get lost, or something terrible would surely happen to me on the way there since I don't speak English. He also wants to go, but he can't get away from work now. After a lot of thinking, we decided to send Ana to stay with you for the school year. It will be a good experience for her, and she will have the opportunity to learn the language. Most importantly, she'll be with you at this special time. She is young and doesn't know too much about babies or housework, but she'll learn.

We are all well and miss you terribly. You don't know how much I wish you were here with us for the baby's birth. I know it's going to be hard for you without us. How I wish . . . Well, no point in going on about it. I'll be with you in spirit.

Your sister will arrive in Chicago on June 5, in just a couple of weeks. I'm enclosing her flight number, etc. Be sure to be at the airport. She's only fifteen and would be terribly frightened to find herself alone. It's a long trip, and your father is so worried. He wishes he had not agreed to it. I didn't tell you about her trip until everything was ready so you wouldn't be disappointed.

With all my love,
Mother

What joy! I wish I could dance and jump up and down, but I don't dare. I read the letter again.

I can't wait to share my news with Pablo. Excitement takes over with such force that I move around the apartment aimlessly. "Work!" I exclaim. I should have been at my desk ten minutes ago. I pick up my purse and leave.

When I come home in the evening, I find Pablo looking out the window.

"I was getting worried. You're usually here by six."

"I was late for work and had to finish a long job. Guess what? My sister Ana is coming to stay with us for a school year and to help when the baby comes."

"That's wonderful. I bet you're excited. I know how much you miss your family. Why Ana instead of María?"

"I don't know. María probably has a boyfriend and would rather stay there. Ana isn't at that stage yet."

We go on and on about it, making plans to arrange the apartment for all of us. I'm glad we have now a larger dwelling with a sofa bed for my sister. We bought a small crib and have collected a lot of baby items. A few neighbors got together and gave me a baby shower two weeks ago. I don't have to worry about clothes since family and friends have sent so many.

June 4

These two weeks have disappeared in a jiffy. There has been so much to do. Saturday's picnic was lovely. Tomorrow is the day my sister comes. We're going to the airport in the morning to meet her. The anticipation is unbearable. It has been so long—actually a whole year—since I've seen anyone from my own family.

My back hurts. I've been cleaning and organizing all day, working in slow motion. I take off my shoes and lie on the sofa. I need a rest before I finish cooking dinner.

"Marcela, are you all right?"

I open my eyes. Pablo is standing there, looking at me. I lift myself to a sitting position. "I'm okay, but very tired. Did you just come home?"

"Yes. Stay there, I'll fix us soup or something. You've done more than you should in the last few days."

"I already made sauce for noodles. Just help me cook the pasta." Still groggy, I drag my bulk to the kitchen.

I've learned to make sauces using soups. I add spices, parsley, and Italian seasoning to a mushroom soup, a little water and milk, and presto! I have a sauce—no more red pepper on my pasta. I add a salad, and soon we have an edible dinner we truly enjoy.

"I'm going to bed as soon as I wash the dishes. I feel strange."

"Does anything hurt?"

"No, it's just . . ." I don't know how to explain the uneasiness and general discomfort. Like Pablo says, I've pushed myself beyond endurance.

He helps clear the table, gets out his books, and settles in for a long evening, like he does almost every night, going to bed past midnight. I'm used to it by now. It's so much better in this apartment where I can go to our dark room to sleep.

I manage to clean the kitchen in spite of my backache and uneasiness. I go back to the sofa and turn on the television. I need to gather some energy and relax so I can go put on my nightclothes.

"Ouch!"

"What is it?" Pablo runs to me.

"I don't know. A sharp pain went all across my stomach. It's okay now." I put my hand over my big belly. The baby is kicking furiously.

Pablo stares at me in terror. "The baby isn't supposed to come for a week or two, right?"

"The twelfth is the due date, remember? Go back to your books. I guess I ate too much. Don't stay up late. We need to leave for the airport by nine." Please, little baby, wait a couple of days.

CHAPTER XXIX

CHILDBIRTH, AN INEXPLICABLE miracle of life, happened to me three times, bringing a girl and two boys into our lives. The lack of understanding and preparation for this earthshaking event is an understatement of my ignorance at the time of the birth of my firstborn.

There is no job description for parenthood, for we enter into it blindly. Millions of women have delivered babies since the beginning of time, and millions of babies have survived, affirming that a guardian angel is assigned to every human being, or else most of us would not be here. My children probably came with more than one angel.

Some women have easy deliveries. Not me. I went on forever, and then I was so weak I had to lean against the wall to walk. Since my children were born in the United States, away from my family's help, which would have made it easier, I had to manage with only the help of my husband and good friends. The birth of our first child is engraved in my mind in a minute-to-minute replay.

June 4

I can't sleep, so I turn on the television and find a movie with John Wayne, one of those cowboy movies Pablo likes. Half an hour goes by, and another shooting pain makes me curl as far as I can go. I don't say anything, deciding to wait and see if the pain and cramps come back and how far apart they are.

I don't know what's going on in the movie anymore. My suitcase is almost packed. Quietly, I walk to the bathroom and get my toothbrush and other toiletries and stuff them in the bag and then go back to the couch.

Fifteen minutes later another cramp leaves me breathless. I time them for an hour. They are coming harder and harder, about ten minutes apart now.

I stand. "Pablo, I think we need to go to the hospital. I'm having contractions every ten minutes."

"Are you sure? Sit down." He doesn't seem to know what to say or do.

"I'm sure. Oh, ayyyy!" I scream. This time the pain is so intense I fall back on the sofa and twist.

Pablo pales. "We better go." He walks from the kitchen to the main room and back two or three times.

"My bag is ready in the bedroom. I'll get my purse and put on my shoes while you get it."

By the time we get to the car, I have had another horrible cramp. I'm glad the hospital isn't far away. I look at my watch. It's about ten thirty. I put my hands under my stomach, hoping to diminish the severity of the next cramp. Every couple of minutes Pablo asks how I feel. "I hurt and I'm frightened," I answer every time.

A woman at the hospital's admitting desk asks a million questions. I can't think about anything. My name would have faded from my mind if she had asked me instead of Pablo. I suddenly remember we registered weeks ago. I ask her to look for my file. I don't know how my jumbled mind provided me such vital information. Another cramp takes me away to the land of pain.

A nurse appears with a wheelchair. Pablo follows. After rolling from hallway to hallway, she stops in front of a small room where I'm put to bed. The nurse says something I can't make out and leaves.

A young doctor comes in, asks Pablo to wait outside, and then examines me. "You are just beginning to dilate. It's going to be a long night. Try to relax. We'll be calling your doctor as soon as you are ready."

I don't know how many hours I've been here. Doctor and nurses come every so often to examine me. Pablo holds my hand while I scream, which I do every few minutes. I don't know what else to do. He looks worried, and I am desperate. When will this pain end? I pray, close my eyes, and hope for the best.

June 5

I notice a ray of light coming through the blinds. Is it finally morning? It seems like days since I entered this cold, dreary room. Unbearable pain and fear are driving me to the point of losing it. Will I? The thought makes me react, and I try to calm down. I'm hoarse from screaming. Pablo, his eyes red, face pale, and with a worried look, stands by the bed.

"Are you feeling better?"

"No. When is this baby coming? What does the doctor say?" The night doctor stopped talking to me hours ago. I guess it isn't easy to communicate with an out-of-control person.

Pablo takes a wet towel and puts it on my forehead. He has been doing it all night. I don't know if it helps, but there is nothing else he can do. I want my mother so badly. I close my eyes and see her beautiful hazel eyes comforting me. It isn't fair. Why isn't she here?

"The doctor says everything is okay. You're just having a difficult time." Pablo pauses for a moment. "We have a big dilemma. The baby may take a long time in coming, and your sister arrives in a few hours. I don't know what to do. I don't want to leave you here alone. I wish I knew a way to get word to her or . . ."

"I forgot about her. Of course you have to go. Someone has to be at the airport when she arrives. I'll be okay."

My exhausted body is numb for a few moments. I wait and take a deep breath. The nurses keep telling me that deep breathing helps. "You have to leave now. There is no alternative. It's too late to find someone to help us. You barely have time to drive to Chicago."

Pablo paces the room while hoarse screams emanate from my throat with each excruciating pain. He rushes to my side and then goes back to pacing.

"You're wasting time. Go get her and come right back, but be careful, don't drive fast. I'll survive. My doctor is coming soon. He'll take care of me." I imagine my naive sister, terrified, sitting on her luggage for hours. Who knows what could happen to her?

It takes a lot of convincing for Pablo to decide to leave me. He finally does. What an incredible coincidence for Ana and the baby to arrive the same day. What mocking spirit is playing jokes on us?

A feeling of abandonment creeps over my soul as another intense pain moves in, pushing it aside.

A nurse comes in. "I'm sorry your husband had to leave. He told me to look after you while he's gone. Don't you know someone who can stay with you?" She looks at me with sad brown eyes. "You've been hollering all night. No wonder your voice is almost gone. Bless you, child."

Thinking is difficult in my state of mind. The only person would be Kate Williams. She is a mother and would understand. I hate to bother her though. Should I? "There is a woman who might—but she's probably busy."

The nurse asks me for her telephone number. I can't think of it right now. She'll need to look it up in the telephone directory. I feel another big one coming. I give the nurse the Williamses' name and go back to yelling. My throat hurts, but I can't concern myself with it.

"The doctor will come in a few minutes. I made the call to Mrs. Williams." The nice nurse smiles, holds my hand for a moment, and leaves.

About an hour later Kate walks in. I am ready to give up. I don't know what I could give up since I continue struggling. The ER doctor said I'm dilating, and my regular doctor will be coming soon.

Kate hugs me. "My poor girl. I'm glad you had the nurse call me. She told me about Pablo having to leave. I'm so sorry."

I can't help bawling. "Having a baby is too, too terrible," I manage to say. It's too hard to be strong and brave when you are in so much pain.

"Say whatever comes to mind in Spanish. Don't worry about it, just say it."

She holds my hand and I comply, hoping no one can understand me. I'm not one to say bad words, but I spit every Spanish word that comes to mind.

About two hours later my doctor finally shows up. "You have kept me on the phone all morning, young lady. This baby doesn't want to leave his cozy home, eh?"

I'm not in the mood for jokes. I know he's trying to make me feel better, but it isn't working. "I want the pain to go away. Do something, Doctor, please."

"Now, now, be brave. It'll be over soon. Let's examine you."

I hate for people to talk down to me. I may be young, but I'm not a child. After all, I'm going to be a mother.

"I'll wait outside." Kate touches my arm and leaves.

"I can't endure this any longer." Another cramp stops my complaining.

"You're getting there. Hold on for a little while. Here, suck on this ice. I'll be back soon."

I want to drag him back and force him to take this baby out once and for all, but I don't say anything.

Kate comes back. I can't scream anymore. I twist and moan for the following minutes, hours, days? I can't tell the passing of time.

Kate continues to console me, wet my forehead, and just be here. It seems like hours since Pablo left. Kate has come close to taking my mother's place. I'll never be able to repay her kindness.

The door opens. Pablo and Ana rush in. I'm still twisting, and strange guttural sounds come from my throat. My sister stares at me in terror. She doesn't say anything. From what little I can gather, I believe she's in shock.

"I was afraid we wouldn't be back for the baby's birth," Pablo says.

"I wish it was already over. I'm so glad you're both here."

Kate gets her purse and hugs me. "Now that your family is with you, I'll take my leave."

"Thank you for staying with Marcela. I can't put into words my gratitude. THANK YOU!"

"I couldn't leave her alone. I'm glad I could help." Turning to my sister, she says, "Hi, Ana, I'm happy to meet you. My family thinks a lot of this sweet couple. Welcome. I hope to see you again soon. Pablo, keep me posted, please."

Ana smiles at Kate and says, "Hi." She keeps looking at me as if I were a Martian, not the sister she knew.

I should explain to Kate that Ana doesn't speak English and that she is too shy to answer, but the pain is pressing almost continuously. She leaves, and I go back to my misery.

Doctors and nurses pop in and out. Ana barely talks. Pablo paces, and I continue to groan.

"We're taking you to the delivery room. It's time." A nurse rolls a bed into the room.

Another nurse follows. In minutes they transfer my body, big stomach and all, to the rolling bed.

Pablo reaches to me and says something sweetly that I can't assimilate. Ana walks toward me and stops. I look back and wave.

I stop being afraid, and I don't know why. There is only one thought in my head. I'm on my way to becoming a mother.

CHAPTER XXX

*M*OST OF US *expect wisdom to make an appearance as soon as a baby lands in our arms for the first time. Sometimes this wisdom takes its time showing up.*

I often wonder how my firstborn survived my stupidity. I could have killed my daughter just by feeding her since it never occurred to me that giving a baby the same bottle for days could poison her. She would drink a couple of ounces, and I would keep the bottle in the refrigerator until it was gone, which sometimes took days. This was just one of my many huge mistakes.

I choose to believe that somehow, in spite of it all, and with help from the Creator of these tiny humans, I learned to be an okay mother, according to my children.

June 5

I awaken in a big room. My stomach hurts. It isn't the same pain I had for hours but one that keeps me from moving. Has the baby been born? I touch my belly softly. The big bulk is gone. I remember a room with lots of lights and doctors and nurses with masks. Someone gave me anesthesia, and then I must have gone under.

There are more beds in the room. Why am I with other people? I hear women talking. I want to see my baby. It takes me a while to find the bell since I can't move. Where is Pablo? Why am I with these strangers?

"Here is your daughter. She has been waiting for her mother to wake up." A nurse brings a bundle of white wrappings in her arms and hands it to me.

I lift my head and look inside, finding a tiny baby with lots of hair, combed in some kind of curl on top. My heart jumps. It's a girl. Is she really mine? How can it be? My eyes fill with tears. She is so tiny, and I was so big. I wonder why.

The nurse says, "I've not seen a baby with so much hair since I've been working here, so we had fun styling it for you. Isn't she precious?"

I nod, unable to speak.

"I'll leave her with you for a little while so you can get acquainted. I'll be back for her soon."

"Why can't she stay with me all the time?"

The nurse tells me I need my rest, and the baby needs care at the nursery. She'll bring her to me when she needs to eat, about four times a day and a couple of times at night if I breastfeed her.

I didn't think about that. Of course I'll do it. So many things to learn. "Why am I in this room with other women?"

"I don't know. You'll have to ask your family. Most rooms at this hospital have two to four beds. Your husband asked me to tell you he'll be back soon. He took your sister home. Now I have to take other babies to their mothers."

I cuddle my tiny red-faced doll, talk to her, and try to nurse her, but she keeps on sleeping, not paying much attention to me.

The woman across the room doesn't want to look at the baby the nurse brings to her. "Look how pretty she is." The nurse puts the child on the bed.

"I didn't want another child. I already have four." The woman looks the other way. She finally gives in and takes her baby but doesn't look at it.

I feel sorry for both. Hopefully she changes her mind with time. How could she not love her own flesh?

June 7

It has been a couple of days since I gave birth, and I still feel too weak to walk a few steps. There was no way to change to a private room, so I do the best I can. The semester is almost over, so Pablo has more time to visit me. He is bringing my sister today.

"Happy birthday, Ana. I'm sorry I'm not able to celebrate your birthday. We'll do something in a couple of weeks."

"Kate Williams invited us to her house. She is baking a cake for me." For the first time Ana looks relaxed, even excited.

We talk about how scary it must have been for her to find me in such a state and then having to deal with being at the apartment by herself. I'm glad Kate is throwing a little party for her. This kind woman is a special person.

"It was scary all right. I didn't know that having a baby was so painful. I don't want to go through that."

I don't comment. What can I say? Her time will come. "I can't wait to go home. The doctor says it'll be soon."

Ana is in a hurry to go to her party. She tells me Kate is waiting and walks out of the room.

Pablo lingers for a moment, gives me a kiss, and leaves with Ana.

June 10

I know I'm going to faint as we walk up to our apartment. Pablo is carrying our new daughter. I grab the wall, the banister, and whatever I can hold on to until we reach the door to our domicile.

I look at the tiny creature Pablo puts in the crib. She is pretty, and she is ours. I feel my chest swell with pride.

The nurses liked to comb her hair in a big curl on top of her head. This time they must have put a little gel or something to make it stay. She's not so red anymore and has the littlest nose I've ever seen. I put my arm around her body. She's wet.

"Kate brought all these diapers." Ana opens a package.

I hold a big piece of soft fabric on the bed, with no clue of what to do. It never occurred to me to find out how to fold a diaper and how to put it on a baby.

When you think you are ready to face the different tasks in life, something happens to let you know there is still much to learn.

Pablo volunteers, tries different ways, and gives up.

I'm the mother, so I should know better. I take the cloth, fold it twice and attempt to put it on her. By the time I'm ready to use the safety pin, the diaper is around her neck. She doesn't like it and begins to cry.

Ana steps back. "Don't look at me. I don't know anything about babies."

I ask Pablo to call Chris. She doesn't have children, but her sister does. She might know.

Chris turns out to be an expert. She makes me fold a diaper several times until I get the hang of it.

July 24

I can't believe my ignorance. Shouldn't mothers have a sixth sense about taking care of their young? I'm in doubt of my motherly skills, and I'm ashamed to mention the very stupid things I do every day. Pablo and Ana are clueless, so they try to help in other ways. I call Kate, Chris, and Joanne and write letters to Mama asking for help. I'm adamant I will become a good mother. It'll take time, but I know I will.

The baby cries a lot. She doesn't nurse much, so the doctor orders me to give her a bottle. I still try to do both. It takes her two or three days to finish one bottle. She sleeps little, and so do I.

Other than lack of sleep, I'm finally feeling like myself again. It's about time since little Tanya is almost two months old. Her baptism was a couple of weeks ago. I'll be going back to work in about two weeks. I'll be working evenings instead of afternoons so Ana or Pablo can take care of the baby. Ana will start school soon, and Pablo will be back to his heavy schedule.

"Hi, pretty baby. You're nice and clean, so you're going to take a good nap." I pray she does. I could sure use one. I spent half the night rocking her.

I hear the phone ring. No one is home to answer it. Ana went to the store across the street. I have finished bathing the baby, and I'm dressing her. I put a shirt on her, leave her on top of the table, and rush to get the telephone. As I say hello, I hear a scream as something hits the floor. I throw the phone and run.

Oh my God! What did I do? How could I have been so stupid? I pick up my sobbing, terrified baby from the floor and hold her until she calms down.

I look at every inch of her body. She seems alert and moves arms and legs. I pray she didn't hit her head. I rock her for a long time, afraid to put her to sleep.

I don't tell anybody about the baby's fall. What mother leaves her baby on top of a table? I thought she was too small to move from where I left her. I look at her every hour for several days until I decide she's okay. Her guardian angel must have cushioned the fall.

August 10

"Pablo, pay attention! Give her a bottle in about an hour. Make sure she's breathing okay when she goes to sleep. Change her diaper when she awakes." I hate to leave her, even with her father. If her mother, who should know better, has made so many dangerous mistakes, what can I expect from anybody else?

Pablo sits with Tanya on his lap and, in a somewhat annoying voice, tells me not to worry. He plans to pick me up after work since he doesn't want me to walk alone at night.

In an uneasy mood I walk to work. I enter the building, wanting to turn around and go back to my little girl. It's hard to concentrate while I worry about Tanya. Time goes by too slowly. I can't wait to go back home.

Alicia stops by my desk. "It's so nice to have you back. I've missed you. How is that precious baby of yours? She must be real cute now." Alicia had stopped by the apartment to see the baby the first week after I left the hospital.

"She doesn't sleep much, but she's doing well."

"I'll also be working in the evenings for a few months," Alicia tells me. "We are saving for a down payment for a house when my husband and I graduate, so we'll be working together again."

August 27

Working until late and not sleeping much at night is catching up with me. It has been a few weeks since I went back to work, and

I'm on automatic pilot. I go from morning to night doing what I have to do. Ana has learned a little cooking, which helps. At first she didn't know how to go about anything. She was "me" when I first came, times two.

I recently began to take care of Mario, a six-month-old baby from my building. I didn't want to do it, but his mother, who works while her husband goes to school, begged me to help her. She brings him about eight in the morning. If I'm lucky and the two babies take a nap, I take one too.

Alicia and I are on our way to the cafeteria. We are back to drinking hot chocolate almost every evening at break time.

I ask her to go ahead. I'm going to put some cold water on my face. I need to wake up.

I can't keep my eyes open. I go to the ladies' room and splash water on my face. There is a covered trash can by the door. I can't resist the temptation to sit on it for a moment. I lean against the wall and close my eyes.

"Marcela, Marcela, wake up. Are you okay?"

"What? I must have fallen asleep. How long have I been here?"

"At least half an hour," says Alicia. "I waited for you at the cafeteria, and after ten minutes I went back to work. Since you didn't come back, I began to worry. You can't continue doing so much. You're making yourself sick."

She's right, but I don't know what else to do. We need the money, so I have to work. It won't be for long. Pablo will finish his master's by Christmas. Most importantly, I need for Tanya to sleep at night so I don't go around falling asleep on trash cans.

CHAPTER XXXI

*A*S OFTEN STATED, *house chores and cooking have been a thorn in my side since day one. They have also been part of my daily life since arriving in the United States.*

These chores, hard enough for me without children, became almost unbearable when taking care of them. After a lot of complaining and struggling, I have managed to come to terms with these inevitable tasks. I thank God for the women who have helped me keep my house in order throughout the years. They don't know how they have contributed to my sanity. This luxury was not possible during those first years, when I needed help the most.

It's amazing how experience turns a person into an expert. I've learned a few tricks along the way to make life easier. I wish I had known a few of them back when I drove myself into a frenzy by trying to do everything at once.

September 7

Motherhood is a complex task I struggle with every day. It requires lots of energy, patience—a virtue I don't possess—creativity, and of course love. The lack of one or more of these qualities could send a woman to run away from home. There is so much to learn and do. It's overwhelming.

Tanya was four months old two days ago. I'm dressing her in a red wool outfit Mama sent me. It's a cool September Sunday. She looks adorable.

"Small children shouldn't go to church. It's hard on them and on us," Pablo says.

"It'll be years before she is old enough to behave. We can't stop going to church that long. God can't be put on hold. Here, Ana, will you put on her sweater while I wash the dishes?"

"They can wait till later." Pablo doesn't worry about this kind of task.

I hate to leave dirty dishes in the sink. Stubbornly, I run to the kitchen and begin to wash them.

A few minutes later Pablo comes in, holding little Tanya. "You'll drive yourself crazy this way."

He's probably right, but I keep quiet and finish the job, before leaving for church.

An hour or so later we're back home. On Sundays I try to cook something a little more special even though my recipe repertoire is very small. I'm trying out a ground beef casserole recipe I cut out from a magazine.

I put the baby to bed and go to the living room to join the others. "It's such a pretty day, we should go out this afternoon."

"Let's do it." Ana jumps at the opportunity to get out of the house. She has been struggling with the language at school.

Pablo lifts his head from the book he's reading. He agrees.

Ana sets the table, and soon we are deep in conversation about family and events. We do this every so often. It keeps us close to the family back home and to those wonderful occasions we miss and love to relive.

Summer is almost over, and cool weather has been playing a peekaboo game lately. We have been in Urbana for about a year. Sometimes I think it has been a century ago since I left my country. In a few months our stay here will be over. Pablo has been talking about going to MIT to take a few courses before we go back to South America. I think Boston is a great city with so many places to see. I liked it a lot when we went to visit our friends last Christmas.

"Oh no! I forgot the casserole." I run to the kitchen and open the oven. The space between racks is too small, so without a second thought, I lift the upper rack with my bare hands. A screeching scream from inside my being resounds throughout the apartment.

"What happened?" yells Pablo as he stumbles to the kitchen.

The pain is horrible. I can see shreds of my skin stuck to the oven rack. "Do something, please, do something!" I extend my burnt hands toward him.

"What did you do now?" He looks at my hands in horror. "Let's go to the university clinic."

Ana's frightened face appears behind Pablo. "I'll stay with the baby."

"I can't stand the pain. I'm going to put my hands in cold water."

"No. We don't know if that's the right thing to do. Let's go." Pablo grabs my arm and rushes me out.

The clinic sends us to the nearest hospital emergency room. The pain and burning is unbearable. I keep my hands up, terrified to touch anything.

At the hospital, a young doctor carefully spreads a cold ointment on my red raw hands and lets me know it'll take a week or two before I can use my hands.

I turn my face. I don't want to look.

He tells me I'll have to wear special gloves to keep the medication from rubbing away. He puts the gloves on my burnt extremities. I bite my lips.

If I could use my hands, I would write a million times, "Think before you act."

September 21

It's getting cold, and it's harder for me to get up in the morning. My hands finally feel better. The first week, I was miserable. I needed help to get dressed and to do the simplest tasks. Ana and Pablo took care of Tanya, and Mario's mother had to find someone else for the time being. I kept my hands bathed in ointment and the gloves on most of the time.

Like everything in life, the pain subsides in a few days, and by the end of the second week, the healing process is almost complete. Now I'm back to being in charge of most everything around me, including work and Mario.

Tanya still doesn't sleep much, so I'm always sleepy. I work from six to midnight four times a week, giving me little time to rest.

Tanya has been uneasy all morning. She seems to be coming down with a cold. I feed her lunch, give her an aspirin, and put her down for a nap. To my surprise she goes right to sleep, and Mario is asleep in his playpen. I wait a few minutes and then go straight to bed. Soon I'm lost to the world.

Pounding at the door and Tanya's crying bring me back from the deepest sleep. I sit on the bed for a moment. Urgent pounding continues. I get up and run to the door. Ana and Chris stand in front of me.

"Why didn't you open the door for me when I came home from school?" Ana says between sobs. "You don't want me here anymore. I want to go back home."

"What time is it? When did you knock? Come in. I didn't hear you knock."

Chris sits on the sofa. "I told her you were either not home or didn't hear the knock. She was very upset when she came looking for me."

"Thank you, Chris, for helping once again."

Ana continues crying. "I waited and knocked for a long time. I knew you were home and didn't want to open the door."

"How can you think that? You don't know how wonderful it is for me to have you here. Because I don't sleep much with my daughter awake half the night and work and everything else, I guess I went into a sleeping coma. You're upset because you have been homesick and I haven't had time to pay enough attention to you with so much going on. I've gone through terrible homesickness myself. I know how you feel. I didn't hear a thing until now. I'm sorry."

After my rambling speech, Ana calms down. I promise to make her favorite dessert this weekend, Boston cream pie. Chris stays for a few minutes and leaves. I need to pay more attention to my sister. She's still a child. I give Ana and Tanya big hugs before I leave for work.

September 22

Tanya's cold is not better. She coughs and sneezes a lot. I'm glad I'm not working this evening so I can stay with her. Since I have the time, I decide to bake Ana's dessert. It's Friday, so she'll have it a day earlier. With an easy recipe on the box, baking it shouldn't be too hard.

Dinnertime is special tonight. Ana seems happy. Pablo is thrilled about his grades. He has managed to keep an A average for over a year. I don't know how he has done it in another language. All those sleepless nights are paying off.

Pablo plays with Tanya. She laughs and goes into a coughing fit. "She seems to have a cold." Pablo puts her down.

"Yes, she has had it since yesterday. I'm going to give her an aspirin and put her to bed."

When I come back, I sit down at the table where Pablo and Ana are eating a second helping of the cake. I'm ready to do likewise. "She must really be sick. That child never goes to sleep at night this easily."

"Does she have a fever?" Pablo looks worried.

"I don't think so." Before I put her to bed, I checked her forehead.

It feels good to go to bed early and in a quiet room. I read for a few minutes and doze off.

A noise buzzes around in my head. I'm so sleepy I don't want to acknowledge it. The sound goes on until I'm awake. It's coming from Tanya's crib. She's making horrible sounds from her throat.

I turn the light on. "Pablo, Pablo, wake up. The baby is sick, listen to her."

Soon the three of us are sharing panic in front of the crib.

I come to my senses and pick up my child. She's red and hot. I look at my watch. It's one in the morning.

"We have to do something." Pablo seems to find some solace in pacing.

I give her another aspirin and lay her down, but she doesn't get any better, and she's having difficulty breathing. "I'm calling Mario's mother. If she doesn't know what to do, we're taking her to the hospital." I hate to call anybody at this time, but I have no choice. We need to do something fast.

I hang up the phone and rush to get my little one out of the crib. I undress her and carry her to the tub. Mario's mother thinks

Tanya might have the croup. She asked me to bathe her in cool water to get the fever down. She's bringing a vaporizer for her breathing.

After several minutes, Tanya's temperature comes down from 104 degrees to 102. I take her out of the tub, wrap her in a towel, and turn the shower on as hot as it gets. The bathroom fills with warm moisture. My wise neighbor provided me with this remedy, to be followed by the vaporizer. Tanya's breathing seems to improve.

I can't wait for the sun to come out. It's five in the morning. I've spent all night rocking little Tanya, the vaporizer close to her face while I ponder the difficulties of parenthood.

She would not let her father or aunt hold her. I guess only a mommy will do at this time, even a mommy who's a slow learner. At eight in the morning, I call the doctor's office. I'm dizzy from lack of sleep but happy to have overcome my baby's first serious illness.

CHAPTER XXXII

FEELING LOST AND alone happens to most of us at one time or another. This familiar feeling was most prevalent on the day we arrived at MIT in Boston for Pablo to continue his studies. Never in a million years could we have predicted such a day. We think these extraordinary events can only happen in the movies or to other people, but never to us.

I always wonder if it is something we do or don't do that puts us in harm's way or in the strangest of circumstances, or if God gives us these happenings in order to help us grow, learn how to fend for ourselves, and become resourceful, or if these events happen to some of us as a fluke because we are where we are at the time.

For whatever reason, we go through these occurrences by radar. I continue to believe heavenly beings take us by the hand, or we wouldn't be able to survive some of the travails that spring up along the way.

December 29

October and November were busy, uneventful months. December is about over. We spent our second Christmas away from home with our surrogate parents, the Williamses. It was a nice and different Christmas, not celebrated on Christmas Eve but the next day, as is the custom in this country.

We'll soon be leaving for Boston. I stopped working before Christmas. Pablo was accepted at MIT to take the courses he wants before we go back home in June. We'll be in Boston for a school semester. I'm looking forward to big-city life for a while and then *home*. Just thinking about it gives me such pleasure. I can't stop the desire to scream and yell, "I'm going home soon!"

We are in the middle of packing. "Ana, how do you feel about being in a high school in Boston? It's a big city and it'll be different."

"It'll be interesting, and I'm excited about it, but I'm also afraid. The school here is just a couple of blocks away, and I'm already used to it. Everyone has been nice to me. I don't know if it'll be the same in Boston."

"I'm sure it'll be fun for you."

Tanya is playing with two pots she bangs together, disturbing my thinking. She likes pots and pans better than toys. I can't believe we're leaving this place in a couple of days. It's sad to leave the Williamses, Chris, and all the friends we have here.

Ana stops her packing for a moment. She looks pensive. I know why she's sad. It isn't so much the school but the tall and good-looking engineering student she met a couple of months ago. He studies at one of the universities in South America and is on a one-year abroad program at the university here. They have gone out to movies and university events a few times. I think she likes him a lot. Her mind is somewhere else. Her big brown eyes have a melancholy look. I leave her alone with her thoughts.

I can't believe what the Williamses did. They really are unique. They bought from us the fan we have in the bedroom and most of the items we can't take with us. I know they don't need any of it. They just want to help us out with some money. These wonderful people have been such a blessing to us.

I hope Pablo gets here soon. There is so much to do and pack. He's at the university, doing some paperwork for his degree. Too bad we won't be here for the graduation ceremony. His diploma will be mailed to him.

January 5

We are finally on our way. Pablo takes a deep breath as he accelerates out of the city, our home for the last year and a half.

It's cold. I embrace myself and look back.

We keep silent for a while, engrossed in thought. The last few days were really nice. Chris invited us to dinner one night. Some of the neighbors got together and threw a small party for us. The Williamses prepared a wonderful meal last night. A few of my coworkers invited me to lunch. It was hard to say good-bye to all of them. We have said good-bye to many nice people in different parts of this country. I wonder about the blue boy and his family. Will he make it? They left some weeks ago, and probably we'll never know what happens to him. I'll even miss Mario. He is such a good-natured boy.

"It's going to be a long and cold trip," Pablo says in a serious tone. "We have to drive slowly because of ice and snow, besides all the cargo we stuffed in the car. I don't know how the car is moving at all."

Luggage seems to be part of our name now. The traveling bassinet the Williamses gave us, with the baby sleeping inside, barely fits between the back and driver seats. Ana sits by the window, a suitcase in between the bassinet and her. There are bags on the floor and everywhere else we could shove them.

I don't know what to say, so I don't comment. Pablo has complained about the luggage for so long. I stopped worrying about it. Instead of having less, now we have the baby and all her stuff and Ana and her belongings. Poor Pablo, but it's like my mother says, "When you don't like the soup, you get two bowls."

We drive and drive, and then we drive over what seems to be the same freeways and snowbanks until it gets dark. We have stopped at a couple of roadside restaurants to grab a bite and warm up. It's getting dark. We exit and head to a motel we saw advertised twenty miles back.

Pablo deposits a couple of bags on one of the beds in the room where we'll spend the night. "We'll have to get up early. I want to get to Boston tomorrow before it gets dark."

Ana helps me carry the bassinet. I'm hungry. "Let's eat dinner and go to bed."

Ana looks out the window. "I didn't see anything but this lone motel. Is there a town close-by?"

"Probably, but we don't want to go far. We'll find something here." Pablo looks tense and tired. "I'll go and ask."

Dinner ends up to be a few packages of chips from the motel's vending machine, peanuts, and soft drinks. I'm glad I brought enough canned milk and baby food for Tanya. With our stomachs complaining for lack of nutrition, we go to sleep.

January 6

The drive to Boston turns into a blur. Naked trees and white stuff, which fascinated me when I first saw it, bores me now. It has been snowing for a while, but it seems to be coming harder. We can barely see.

"Look, there is the city," I say, relieved at the sight of the place where this long journey will end, a trip so different from a year ago when everything was exciting and new, with the exception of Douglas, our nightmare passenger. It's still exciting, but this time it's more the prelude of the expected homecoming.

I hope the woman from MIT housing found something for us so we don't have to go to a hotel tonight. We need to get settled right away.

Pablo eases his tight grip on the steering wheel. We drive slowly through roads and then streets until we reach the Beacon Hill area. There is ice on the ground, and fresh snow is falling harder and harder. Suddenly the car begins to slide as we approach a busy avenue.

"I can't control the car," Pablo yells in panic.

The car zigzags and somehow ends up hitting the sidewalk, stopping a few inches from the traffic. It happens so fast I don't have time to react, but I'm sure glad we're not rolling aimlessly.

Pablo gets out to inspect the damage. "There is only a small dent on the bumper. I'm going to move it over by the curb and go find a telephone. It doesn't look very good with all the snow that is falling. We need a place as soon as possible."

I feed Tanya while Pablo makes his call. She has been crying for a while. Surprisingly, she has behaved pretty well during the trip. A moving car seems to have a soporific effect on her.

"Weren't you afraid?" Ana's face is ashen.

"I didn't have time. Were you?"

"I thought we were going to crash into two or three cars in that avenue."

"Relax, nothing happened. We'll soon be settled someplace." I lay Tanya back in the bassinet and put on my jacket.

It is terribly cold. Since the engine is not running, the heater isn't either. The snow accumulation begins to worry me. It's coming so fast it'll soon be over the tires.

"We are stuck." Pablo rushes inside the car and turns the engine on. "I called from a drugstore around the corner. The woman from housing says she doesn't know how she's going to go home herself much less go with us anywhere. According to her, this is the worst snowstorm in twenty years. She advises us to get a hotel for a couple of days."

Why do these things happen to us? What are we going to do now? Fear chills me with more intensity than the bitter cold outside.

Most of the traffic vanishes. Are we going to freeze inside the car? There is no way to drive it anywhere now. The snow is up to the hood of the car. I don't say what's in my mind. No one does. Tanya cries. I wrap her with a blanket.

Pablo turns his head to me. "We can't sit here until we are so cold we can't move."

I know we have to do something, but my mind is blank.

Pablo opens the door. "Let's see if there is a hotel or something around here."

We leave Ana in the car with the baby and tell her to keep as warm as she can.

The snow is so high that walking is almost impossible. It takes us a long time to advance a few steps. The snow is too heavy, and soon my legs are stuck.

Pablo tries to help me, but neither of us can move. Necessity is the mother of invention, I've always heard. I grab one leg with my hands, pull it out, and take a step. Then I do the same with the other leg. It takes a while to move them, but it works.

We see on the window across the street an "Apartment for rent" sign.

Pablo's face lights up. We struggle to cross the street, pushed by sheer eagerness to find a warm place to stay. *You don't want us to freeze to death, Lord. Please help us,* I pray. I look at the buildings surrounding us. Years ago they must have been the elegant homes of Boston's wealthy. I remember seeing this neighborhood in a movie. How could I've predicted I would one day find myself in such a place, standing in front of one of the houses, in the strangest of circumstances?

After knocking on the door for what seems an eternity, a stern-faced man finally opens it.

"We just arrived in town and find ourselves stuck in the snow. We need the apartment you have for rent." I don't take time to say the right words. I can't feel my hands or feet. I'm desperate. "My sister and our baby are freezing in the car. We need a place right now."

"What do you do? Where do you come from? I don't rent my apartments just like that."

Pablo turns red. I hit him with my elbow. It isn't the time for hurt feelings. "I just finished my master's at the University of Illinois, and I'm coming to study at MIT."

The man doesn't ask us in. "So you're a student. How are you going to pay the rent? Students don't have money."

"I have a Fulbright Scholarship. We have enough money to pay for the rent. We don't know anyone here. There is no way we can go to a hotel or anywhere else in this weather. We'll be very grateful if you let us have the apartment."

I am proud of Pablo, proud of me. We have come a long way since we left our country.

It takes a lot of begging, tears, and the guilt I put on the man by telling him he will be responsible and will carry this guilt for the rest of his life if we turn up frozen tomorrow. He finally breaks down and makes us sign a six-month lease. How I wish our friend Max and his family were still here.

We find Ana and the baby already looking blue. Pablo's lips are also blue, and I don't feel mine. I rub Tanya's small hands. They are like ice. Wrapped in everything we find, and taking along with us whatever few items we can carry to our new living quarters, we fight sleet and snow as we push and crawl the two blocks separating us from the freezing cold that would have killed us, to a warm apartment we have not seen. Tonight we worry about thawing our bodies. Tomorrow we'll worry about the car and the many trivialities of life.

CHAPTER XXXIII

*F*EW HAPPENINGS COMPARE *with the excitement of going back to your native land, to family and friends after a long separation. There was no reason to believe that we wouldn't be staying in our own country for the rest of our lives. As I suspected, it must have been written in the book of life that we would not grow old in the land of our ancestors.*

Those two years in the United States had been an incredible experience; Pablo had acquired his master's, so we were ready to start life as it should be, according to my family. There was no way to know Pablo would begin collecting graduate degrees as if it were a pastime, and within two years, we would be back to the country we later adopted.

January 6

I've stopped being surprised at the many strange turns in my life. In a slow learning process, I've learned to face them and go on.

Dripping ice and snow, we enter a large room with a small kitchen at one end and a bathroom at the other. I'm glad to see furniture since it didn't occur to either of us to ask about these essential items. We would have had to sleep on the floor otherwise. Still, it would have been better than in a freezing car.

The terrifying scene in my mind of a car with four frozen bodies pushes me to my knees in grateful prayer. It could have easily happened.

There is a double bed, a sofa, a chair, and a small table with four chairs. Ana will have to sleep on the sofa. There is no food to eat or way to go get anything. Asking the landlord for help is out of the question. I feed Tanya the last can of milk and cuddle with her by the heater until we are able to move our limbs. Using some of the clothing we have hauled, we crawl in bed and soon forget the cold world outside and our growling stomachs.

January 14

It takes us a week to get organized. There is no place to park the car, so we leave it in whatever parking space we find on the street. The lack of privacy is getting to us. Pablo began classes two days after we arrived, and he is finding it difficult to study while Tanya cries and Ana and I talk, cook, or go about living. By the second week, we're ready to explode.

Pablo is trying to concentrate over Tanya's wailing. "Marcela, this is not working out. Four people can't live in one room. We're going to have to find another place."

I reminded him that we signed a contract, and the landlord will make us pay for the months we agreed to stay. We can't afford that. It's hard enough to survive with the money we have now.

We've been avoiding the fact that, without me working, we'll soon run out of cash. The scholarship will only pay for rent. I need to work full-time since we need to find someone who can take care of Tanya, and a part-time job would only pay for a babysitter. Finding a job like the one I had in Illinois doesn't seem an option.

I ask Pablo to try a little longer and to go to the library to study. This is a good location. Even though it's inconvenient for all of us, it was miracle that we found this place in the snowstorm.

We agree to give it a try before going through another begging session with the landlord. We have already made him unhappy for asking him not to freeze us during the day and burn us at night. We have no control of the heating unit.

"I can't go to school by myself. I don't know how to get the right bus. I'll get lost," Ana says. Today is her first day of classes.

"It isn't that difficult. You take the bus a block from here and get off at the fourth stop. We went over the directions last night. Pablo would take you, but your school is out of his way."

"I don't want to get lost. What will I do?"

"Okay, let me get Tanya ready, and I'll go with you, but only this time. I can't do this every day. I know this is a big city, and it is scary to face it. But I think you have to learn to at least go to school and to the store by yourself."

It isn't easy to carry a baby around on your hip while trying to balance yourself and not fall on a moving bus. The three of us ride the bus and then walk to school. Two of us go back home, hoping not to have to do it again.

January 30

By the end of the first month, we're ready to pull our hair and are barely short of killing each other. Last night we decided that we couldn't continue living in one room. Today we'll talk to the landlord.

"How ungrateful can you be, after I let you have the apartment when you needed it and begged for it." The man's lips tremble. "You have a six-month binding contract, so don't talk to me about letting you out of it."

"You said the apartment was for one or two people," I dare to say. "You know we had no choice that day. What could we do?"

"That's not my problem. A contract is a contract. If you leave, you pay."

"I know it is, but the reason we are here is for me to go to school," Pablo says. "I can't study. We can't sleep. It has become an impossible situation."

The man crosses his arms and stares at both of us without answering Pablo.

"You won't have any problem renting this apartment, probably for more money than we're paying." I can see his eyes blinking with interest when he hears my words.

It takes a lot more words and arguments to finally convince him to let us out of the lease. We have five days to find another place.

February 8

We found an old furnished apartment on the second floor of a house in Summerville, a suburb of Boston. It's a large place with two bedrooms, a big old kitchen, living room, and spacious hallways. It's nice to have privacy and to be able to close the door when the baby cries, while one of us sees about her. We moved a week ago.

I applied at a couple of companies for a job, and today I have an interview. I hope everything goes well.

A tall, skinny man asks me about my experience, the last job I held, and the reason I left Illinois. He drills me for a while. My answers are as short as I can manage so he thinks my English is good. A few minutes later he walks me to a huge room where dozens of people type away on keypunch machines.

"We have lots of work to be done. Can you start right now?"

"I can work for a couple of hours today. If it's okay with you, I will be ready to start working the day after tomorrow."

"The sooner the better. We need you. I'll send someone to help you get started. Stop by my office before you leave. I need you to sign some papers."

I never expected to be asked to begin work immediately. Pablo is taking care of Tanya. I call him and wait for the next step.

March 15

We have settled in our new life. Ana seems to like her school and soon learns to take the bus. Pablo is busy with his studies, and I'm a full-time everything. Through a neighborhood paper, I found a babysitter for Tanya, a very nice Italian woman who calls my baby *bambina porca* because she gets so messy when she eats.

"I'm late for school. Is this my lunch?" Ana grabs the sandwich I just finished making. Every day I make lunch for all of us.

"You seem happy today. I bet the letter you received yesterday is the reason."

She blushes. "Don't tease me. Why is there a cat on this can of tuna?"

I pick up the can I just used to make our lunches. "Oh my goodness, this is cat food. It says here."

Ana takes her sandwich and, making a face, throws it in the trash can. "The idea that I could have eaten this food nauseates me."

"Me too, especially after the horrible stomach flu I had a week ago." I feel bile coming up my throat.

Ana picks up her books. "I have a couple of dollars. I'll get something at school. See you later."

There is no time to make something else, so we'll just have to make do for lunch. I take the can and dispose of it. No wonder it was so inexpensive. I need to pay more attention when I go shopping.

May 7

Working is boring, and I wish I were doing something else. I'm tired of keypunching. I know I shouldn't complain since this skill has helped us survive. I've made friends at work with a young woman, and she and her husband invited us to their house last weekend. Our outings are usually to the Boston Commons or places where money is not coming out of our pockets. Once in a while we treat ourselves to an inexpensive Italian dinner at a small restaurant we discovered in the area.

Being so busy, I don't notice time going by until May arrives with green trees and flowers everywhere. My heart is ready to burst. We'll be leaving in less than a month. Next Saturday we're going shopping for a few items I want to take back home.

June 5

I want to celebrate Tanya's first birthday with my family, but Pablo won't finish his classes until the tenth of June. We'll still have a party when we go home, but we can't let this important day go by without doing something for her. I bake a cake and invite the Italian babysitter who is crazy about Tanya.

"I'm going to miss my *bambina porca* so much. I hope she likes this book. It's for the trip." The babysitter lets Tanya unwrap a beautiful picture book. She gives her a kiss as she tries to hide her moist eyes.

Tanya is having a great time. She tears wrapping paper and is delighted with what we give her. "Moah, moah," she yells.

I know the word; she wants more cake and more presents. Half of the first piece of cake is on her face and clothes. She knows she is the center of attention and that today she is someone extra special, so she is taking advantage of it.

June 17

I can hardly wait to embrace my parents and the rest of my family, to find the perfect home and become the perfect wife, mother, person, and whatever else I can accomplish. I have waited long enough for all of this to happen.

We're ready to board the plane that will take us from Boston to New York, where we'll change to another airline to go home. It doesn't seem possible that two years have gone by and so many events and happenings have taken place. I'm as nervous as I was when I first boarded the plane to come to this country, and yet I'm not the same naive girl walking to the wrong plane on her way to the unknown. I am a young woman who has faced my uncertain future.

It's raining and the sky is overcast. "I don't like to fly in this weather." I sit by the window and stare at the gray sky.

"I don't like it either." Pablo sits by me. He puts Tanya on my lap.

Ana sits behind us. I feel her looking at me, but she doesn't say anything. We're soon rising toward the dark clouds. The metal bird shakes as it submerges itself inside the weather. Tanya cries and grabs my neck.

"It's all right, baby. Let go of my neck. Please."

She pays no attention and continues crying and holding on to me with all her might. A nasty storm surrounds us. Lightning and thunder amplifies my fear, causing intense pain. I take Pablo's hand. His colorless face says what he doesn't put into words.

"I hate flying." I don't get a response. There isn't much to say.

I pray with all the fervor I can gather. The plane is shaking so bad things begin to fall. The captain orders us to keep our seat belts fastened. I know this plane is about to disintegrate, but I'm afraid to think beyond my fear, fear I see mirrored in most passengers' faces. I close my eyes and rock Tanya to sleep. The plane doesn't stop shaking until we land. So far my flying experience hasn't been too pleasant.

"What a horrible trip," Pablo says, coming back to life as we deplane in New York. He is carrying our sleepy baby and a couple of bags hanging from his shoulders.

I follow him with a few more bags. "I hope the flight to our country is not as bad."

Ana is still mute as she follows us to the Avanta's gate. We don't have a lot of time, so we try to hurry, along with the stuff we're carrying. We have learned a lot about life but not much about traveling light. I hope one day I can manage to walk through an airport, looking sophisticated and cool, with only a purse hanging from my shoulder.

The loudspeaker announces, "*Passengers to . . . prepare to board at gate 6.*"

A young couple walks up. The girl stops and asks in Spanish. "Do you know where gate 11 is? We just arrived from Lima, and we're going to Chicago. We speak little English." She looks lost. He looks confused.

For a moment I go back to the day we arrived. This couple is a version of us on their way to the unknown. "Sure," I say. "Let me tell you where to go." I wish them well.

I see them walk away to follow in our footsteps as we continue with steady step toward the plane. The future awaits us with open arms. I can't wait to fall inside its embrace.

CPSIA information can be obtained at www.ICGtesting.com
Printed in the USA
LVOW08s0348261013

358597LV00002B/139/P